DISCOVERY GUIDE
WITH ALL YOUR HEART

The Faith Lessons™ Series
with Ray Vander Laan

DISCOVERY GUIDE
WITH ALL YOUR HEART

6 FAITH LESSONS™ BY
RAY VANDER LAAN
with Stephen & Amanda Sorenson

THAT THE WORLD MAY KNOW

ZONDERVAN®   FOCUS ON THE FAMILY®

ZONDERVAN.com/
AUTHORTRACKER
follow your favorite authors

ZONDERVAN

With All Your Heart Discovery Guide
Copyright © 2010 by Ray Vander Laan

Requests for information should be addressed to:

Zondervan, *Grand Rapids, Michigan* 49530

ISBN 978-0-310-29117-6

All maps created by International Mapping.

All photos are courtesy of Ray Vander Laan and Mark Tanis.

All illustrations are courtesy of Drew Johnson except pages 25 and 162 (Rob Perry).

All Scripture quotations, unless otherwise indicated, are taken from the Holy Bible, *New International Version®, NIV®.* Copyright © 1973, 1978, 1984 by Biblica, Inc.™ Used by permission of Zondervan. All rights reserved worldwide.

Interior design: Ben Fetterley

Printed in the United States of America

10 11 12 13 14 15 /DCI/ 25 24 23 22 21 20 19 18 17 16 15 14 13 12 11 10 9 8 7 6 5 4 3

CONTENTS

INTRODUCTION

Remember how the LORD your God led you all the way in the desert these forty years.

Deuteronomy 8:2

The exodus of the Hebrew people from Egypt to the Promised Land was more than a compassionate act of divine deliverance. It was God's calling of a people to be his "treasured possession," "kingdom of priests," and "holy nation" who would put him on display for the whole world to see (Exodus 19:4 – 6). God, in effect, took Israel as his bride, and the people promised to do everything God commanded. But vows do not make a marriage, and the Israelites would have to learn to love and obey their God.

That is what the years of discipline and testing in the desert would accomplish. God would live among his chosen people in the tabernacle and through that intimate relationship would mold and shape them to be a people who would be his faithful witnesses to the entire world. Yes, they would fail, and we can learn much from their stubborn disobedience. But they were not failures. The children they parented were ready to take the next step in God's great plan to restore *shalom* to a broken world. They were ready to face the final test: to live in obedience to God's every word and to continue to depend on him for everything they needed in a land blessed with abundance.

Few events are more central to the stories of both the Hebrew text (Old Testament) and the Christian text (New Testament) than the great redemptive acts of God and the people of the exodus. The Hebrew text refers to the exodus theme more than 120 times, plus there are multiple references to related concepts such as manna, water from the rock, Mount Sinai, and the Ten Commandments. The

Christian text mentions Moses eighty-five times and Egypt twenty-nine times.

Yet there is more to the exodus than first meets the eye. The historical account is most useful in understanding God and his desire for the Hebrews to become his witnesses to the world. It is central to understanding why many followers of Jesus considered him to be the prophet like Moses — the Messiah — whom the Lord had promised to send (Deuteronomy 18:17 – 19; Luke 7:16; 24:19 – 20; John 6:14). Jesus often used ideas found in the exodus story, and many of his teachings interpret Moses' words in the Torah. Jesus also positioned his redemptive acts against the background of festivals — Passover, Unleavened Bread, and First Fruits — that are associated with the Hebrews' deliverance from Egypt.[1] And at the deepest level, the exodus story not only provides a background for God's plan to bring Jesus into the world as Messiah, it is one of the first chapters in God's great redemptive story to restore *shalom* — unity, harmony, order — to his broken creation.

Genesis, the first book of the Torah, provides the necessary background for the exodus. Genesis describes God creating a perfect, harmonious universe out of chaos and then describes how sin destroyed that universe, resulting in the loss of harmony in God's creation and the return of chaos. In the stories of the exodus we find the very foundations of the restoration of *shalom* to God's world. Future characters in the Scriptures, including Jesus, build on that foundation. To study these amazing events is to discover that there is really one story — the story of God's redemption. Despite the many failures of God's people in fulfilling their role in that story, God's power has and continues to flow through his flawed human instruments (Jesus excepted, of course) to bring to fruition his plan of redemption.

Thus the exodus is a paradigm for our own experience, and we Christians describe our deliverance in similar language because God delivers us by his mercy and the protecting blood of the Lamb — Jesus Christ. Without the exodus, we would not be who we are — redeemed people delivered by the God of Israel. And without the hardships of the desert experience, we would find it difficult to learn how to live in intimate dependence on his provision and by faithful obedience to his every word.

Clarifying Our Terminology

In this study, the record of God's reclaiming and restoring his broken world is called the Bible, Scripture, or the "text." Having studied in the Jewish world, I believe it is important to communicate clearly how the nature of that inspired book is understood. Although it can be helpful to speak of Scripture in terms of Old and New Testaments, these descriptions also can be misleading if they are interpreted to mean old and outdated in contrast to a new replacement. Nothing, in my opinion, is further from the truth. Whereas the "New Testament" describes the great advance of God's plan with the arrival of the Messiah and the promise of his completed and continuing work, the "Old Testament" describes the foundational events and people through whom God began that work. The Bible is not complete without both testaments; it comprises God's one revelation, his one plan to reclaim his world and restore harmony between himself and humankind. To emphasize that unity, I prefer to refer to the Hebrew text (Old Testament) and the Christian text (New Testament) that together are the inspired, infallible Word of God.

The language of the Bible is bound by culture and time. The geography of the lands of the Bible — Egypt, the desert, the Promised Land — shaped the people who lived there, and biblical writers assumed that their readers were familiar with the culture of that world. Many Christians today, however, lack even a basic geographical knowledge of the region and know even less of the ancient cultures that flourished there. So understanding the Scriptures involves more than knowing what the words mean. It also means becoming familiar with the everyday experiences and images the text employs to reveal God's message so that we can begin to understand it from the perspective of the people to whom it originally was given.

For example, the ancient Hebrew people to whom God revealed himself described their world in concrete terms. Their language was one of pictures, metaphors, and examples rather than ideas, definitions, and abstractions. Whereas we might describe God as omniscient or omnipresent (knowing everything and present everywhere), they would describe him as "my Shepherd." Thus the Bible is filled with concrete images from Hebrew culture: God is our Father and we are his children, God is the Potter and we are the

clay, Jesus is the Lamb killed on Passover, heaven is an oasis in the
desert, and hell is the city sewage dump.

Many of the Bible's images occur first during the exodus: Israel as
God's bride, God as shepherd, the desert as a metaphor for life's difficult experiences, God as living water, God as king, God carrying his
people on eagle's wings, the saving blood of the lamb. The Hebrews
experienced these and many more familiar images as they left Egypt,
spent forty years in the desert, and then entered the Promised Land.

The text frequently describes the people themselves, the descendants of Abraham, as "Hebrews," which probably originated from
the Egyptian *habiru* meaning "dusty ones" (a reference to their
desert origins). Genesis refers to Abraham as "the Hebrew" (Genesis
14:13), and after God gave Jacob the name *Israel*, the text also calls
his descendants *Israelites*. The term *Jew* is not used until much later
in history (see the books of Nehemiah and Esther). We will generally
use the word *Hebrew* because that is how the people were known
in the land of Egypt.

The Hebrew text refers to the land God promised to Abraham as
Canaan or *Israel*. The Christian text calls it *Judea*. After the Second
Jewish Revolt (AD 132 – 135), it was known as *Palestine*. Each of
these names resulted from historical events that took place in the
land at the time the terms were coined.

One of the earliest designations of the Promised Land, *Canaan*,
probably meant "purple," referring to the dye produced from the
shells of murex shellfish along the coast of Phoenicia. In the ancient
world, this famous dye was used to color garments worn by royalty,
and the word for the color referred to the people who produced
the dye and purple cloth. Hence, in the Bible, *Canaanite* refers to
a "trader" or "merchant" (Zechariah 14:21), as well as to a person
from the "land of purple," or Canaan.

Israel, another designation for the Promised Land, derives from the
patriarch Jacob. His descendants were known as the Hebrews as well
as the children of Israel. After they conquered Canaan during the time
of Joshua, the name of the people, *Israel*, became the designation for
the land itself (in the same way it had with the Canaanites). When
the nation split following the death of Solomon, the name Israel was

applied to the northern kingdom and its territory, while the southern land was called Judah. After the fall of the northern kingdom to the Assyrians in 722 BC, the entire land was again called Israel.

During the time of Jesus, the land that had been the nation of Judah was called *Judea* (which means "Jewish"). Because of the influence the people of Judea had over the rest of the land, the land itself was called Judea. The Romans divided the land into several provinces: Judea, Samaria, and Galilee (the three main divisions during Jesus' time); Gaulanitis, the Decapolis, and Perea (east of the Jordan River); and Idumaea (Edom) and Nabatea (in the south). Later during the Roman era (about one hundred years after Jesus' death), the land was called *Palestine.* Although the Egyptians had referred to the land where the Philistines lived as *Palestine* long before Roman times, the Roman emperor Hadrian popularized the term as part of his campaign to eliminate Jewish influence in the area.

Today the names *Israel* and *Palestine* are often used to designate the land God gave to Abraham. Both terms are politically charged. *Palestine* is used by Arabs living in the central part of the country, and *Israel* is used by Jews to indicate the political State of Israel. In this study, *Israel* is used in the biblical sense. This does not indicate a political statement regarding the current struggle in the Middle East, but best reflects the biblical designation for the land.

Present-day Egypt is a beautiful and advanced country, and we do not identify the "Egyptians" of the Bible as identical to the Egyptians of today any more than we would think of the present prime minister of Egypt as the descendant of the Pharaohs. Nor do we draw any political conclusions regarding relationships between the modern state of Israel and the country of Egypt. Throughout the production of this study, we were warmly welcomed and treated with great hospitality in both countries. Our goal is to study God's work with his Hebrew people as he freed them from slavery in ancient Egypt.

Establishing the Historic and Geographic Setting

When studying the exodus of the Hebrews from Egypt, it is natural to ask, "When did that event occur?" Or, to ask it another way, "Who was the Pharaoh 'who did not know about Joseph'?" (Exodus 1:8). There are two basic theories.[2] One places the biblical event in the eighteenth Egyptian dynasty around 1450 BC, during the reign of Pharaohs such as Thutmose (3) or Amenhotep (2).[3] The other places it in the nineteenth dynasty, during the reign of Ramses the Great (1213 – 1279 BC).[4] Significant textual and scientific support exists for each perspective.

Although I have my opinion on the matter, this study does not attempt in any way to argue for one position or the other. The foundational position for this study is that the exodus occurred as the Bible describes it. Since the Bible does not name the Pharaoh (a word similar to *king* in English), God apparently did not believe this fact to be central to his message. However, in much the same way that one studies ancient languages or uses a good commentary, it is helpful to study specific cultural settings in order to better understand the biblical text. Thus this study focuses on Pharaoh Ramses the Great, not because he was the Pharaoh of the exodus but because he is the epitome of all Pharaohs. Whoever the Pharaoh of the exodus was, we can be sure he wanted and tried to become what Ramses the Great would be. By focusing our efforts in this way, we will gain a sense of the culture of the time of the exodus (the two theories are relatively close in time anyway) without the burden of the controversy regarding specific dates.

I hold a similar position regarding the route of the exodus. There are many proposed routes and this study does not seek to support one over another. Rather, I have chosen for this study the type of terrain and culture that would represent whichever route the Hebrews took. If knowing the support for the varying points of view is important to you, other studies should be consulted.

God Reclaims His World through History

From the beginning, God planned to reclaim his world from the chaos of sin. He revealed his plan to restore *shalom* to his creation to Noah, Abraham, Isaac, Jacob, and their families. The books of the Torah, which tell the creation and exodus stories, revealed to the Hebrews who God is, who they were, and who they needed to become. Thus the Torah is God's blueprint describing the role he desires his people to play in his plan of restoration. It forms the foundation of all future acts of God recorded throughout the Bible.

The Hebrews were to be witnesses of God's plan to reclaim his world. Their interaction with the Egyptians and their king, Pharaoh, certainly revealed the nature of the creator of the universe and his desire for his creation (Exodus 8:10; 9:13 – 14). After they reclaimed the Promised Land, the descendants of the Hebrews made God known to many nations as people from all over the world traveled through Israel.

Although his people often have failed in their mission to live righteously and reveal the one true God — *Yahweh*, God continues to use humans as instruments of his redemption. The mission of God's people today is the same one he gave to the ancient Hebrews and Israelites: to live obediently *within* the world so that through us *the world may know that our God is the one true God.* Living by faith is not a vague, otherworldly experience; rather, it is being faithful to God in whatever place and time he has put us.

The message of the Scriptures is eternal and unchanging, and the mission of God's people remains the same, but the circumstances of the people of the Bible are unique to their times. Consequently, we most clearly understand God's truth when we know the cultural context within which he spoke and acted and the perception of the people with whom he communicated. This does not mean that God's revelation is unclear if we don't know the cultural context. Rather, by cultivating our understanding of the world in which God's story was told, we will begin to see it as an actual place with real people and a real culture.

As we explore the Egypt of the Bible and study the people and events in their geographic and historic contexts, we will discover the *who*, *what*, and *where* of the exodus story and will better understand the *why*. By learning how to think and approach life as Amram, Jochebed, Moses, Aaron, Miriam, Joshua, Phineas, and other Hebrews, we will discover that we too experience "Egypt" in our lives. Like the ancient Hebrews, we will discover that it is much easier for God to get us out of Egypt than to get Egypt out of us. And we will discover it is much easier to live by faith and depend on God in the desert than it is to live by faith when it seems that we receive what we need through our own efforts.

The intent of this study is to enter the world of the Hebrews and familiarize ourselves with their culture and the cultures of their day so that we may fully apply the Bible's message to our lives. We will seek to better understand God's revealed mission for the events and characters of the exodus from Egypt and the forty years of training (testing) in the desert so that we, in turn, will better understand God's purpose in Jesus' life and in our lives. Our purpose is to follow God's intent as revealed to Ezekiel:

> *Son of man, look with your eyes and hear with your ears and pay attention to everything I am going to show you, for that is why you have been brought here. Tell the house of Israel everything you see.*

> Ezekiel 40:4

So come, look, and see. Then go and live in such a way that all the world will come to know God as the one, true God.

BUILD ME A SANCTUARY

God's story in the Bible is framed by his desire to live with his beloved people. The story begins in a garden paradise where God walked with his people. It ends in a garden where God's people will live with him forever.

Between these scenes is human history — a story of sin, death, and the resulting broken relationship between God and his created people. But intertwined in human history is the story of God's love and his tireless work to restore that broken relationship. The enslavement of the Hebrews in Egypt, their miraculous deliverance, and their exodus to the Promised Land play a pivotal role in the ongoing restoration of God's relationship with his people.

When the Hebrews walked into the desert of Sinai after crossing the Red Sea, they were at last free from enslavement in Egypt. They were not, however, free from bondage to the beliefs and ways of life they had learned in Egypt. That, in fact, was why God led them into the desert: to test them in order to know what was in their hearts and to teach them to obey his every word (Deuteronomy 8:2 – 3).

In the unknown chaos of the desert they faced hardship and uncertainty. As they walked the difficult path set out before them, they grumbled and at times even questioned God's presence with them. But when they arrived at Mount Sinai, God revealed himself to his people in a new way. In a cloud of glory, darkness, thunder, fire, and lightning, he descended onto the mountain and spoke. He expressed his unending love for them. He promised that if they would live by his every word he would live among them as their loving husband.

Imagine the joy the Israelites felt as they experienced the intimacy of God's presence with them and grew in their relationship with him. Imagine their amazement when God said that he would continue to accompany them on their journey to the Promised Land. No longer would God appear occasionally to a few individuals like the patriarchs and Moses; he would live among them!

To help the Israelites understand the depth of his commitment to live with them and to help them remember that he was present among them, God instructed them to build the tabernacle, a sanctuary for him. The tabernacle was a portable tent shrine that the Israelites would have recognized from the use of such shrines in Egyptian culture. As a familiar cultural form, the tabernacle conveyed a meaningful message that they understood immediately. It was a visual, physical reminder that the sovereign Lord of the universe was with them.

Through the design, construction, and function of the tabernacle, God revealed himself to be unlike any gods his people had known. This study will focus on the purpose, awe, and comfort that the tabernacle — as a symbol of God's constant presence — provided for the Israelites. And it will help those of us who follow Jesus today to better comprehend what it means for us to be the place where God's presence resides.

Opening Thoughts (3 minutes)

The Very Words of God

> *Have them make a sanctuary for me, and I will dwell among them.*
>
> **Exodus 25:8**

Think About It

All of us experience pivotal moments in life when we see as we have never seen before. These moments have the potential to change our lives — what we do, how we see the world, even who we are.

But what happens when these great moments are a few months or years behind us? What keeps these moments alive in our hearts and minds so they continue to make a difference in our lives?

DVD Notes (21 minutes)

How to keep Sinai alive

The Hathor shrine at Timnah

The message of Abu Simbel

God uses the culture to convey his message

DVD Discussion (7 minutes)

1. What are you beginning to discover about the events at Mount
    Sinai and their long-term significance in the lives of the Israel-
    ites? In God's ongoing plan of redemption? In your life?

2. As you viewed the Egyptian temple at Timnah and the tem-
    ple and battle scene carving at Abu Simbel, what sense did
    you gain of the importance of the message these structures
    conveyed to ancient people?

    Why do you think God chose these physical images, and do
    you think they were an effective way to communicate to
    people in ancient times?

3. Briefly review the Israelites' experience with God at Mount
    Sinai. Which aspects of that experience are essential to
    actually living out the kind of relationship with God that he
    offers?

PROFILE OF A CULTURE
The Mining Settlement at Timnah

Located in the Great Rift Valley between the Dead Sea and the Gulf of Aqaba, Timnah is believed to be one of the first major mining areas in the world. The mines there produced copper, which was combined with tin to make bronze, the most valuable metal of the time. Copper production in the area peaked between the 14th and 12th centuries BC, which was roughly the time of the exodus. Copper is still mined in this region.

The Egyptians brought slaves to work the mines and smelting furnaces of Timnah. The workers dug shafts into the ground and then excavated large galleries to mine the copper. Footholds dug into the rock shafts provided access to the galleries—some as deep as thirty meters—that made up one of the most complex tunnel systems of the time. The refined copper was transported to cities along the Nile River.

EVIDENCE OF EGYPTIAN GODS: THE HATHOR SHRINE AT TIMNAH

The temple, or tent shrine, to Hathor at Timnah is evidence of Egyptian influence—where there were Egyptians, there were Egyptian gods. Like other Egyptian temples, the structure has an outer court, inner court, and holy of holies. In the cliff face above the shrine, Pharaoh is depicted bestowing an offering of *ma'at* (indicating that he had maintained harmony in the universe) to Hathor who was known as the protector of miners. As Egyptian power and influence declined in the region, the shrine became a Midianite tent shrine that was similar in design to the biblical tabernacle.

4. Using the map below, locate the cities along the Nile River
    from Abu Simbel to Goshen, then locate the Sinai Peninsula,
    the region of Jebel Musa (the traditional Mount Sinai), and
    Timnah. How far is it from Abu Simbel to Timnah, and what
    does this tell you about the influence of Egyptian culture in
    the world of the Israelites?

    In light of the vast expanse of Egyptian influence (and with
    it the influence of Egyptian gods), what are your thoughts
    about God's desire to live among his people and the way in
    which he chose to express his presence with them?

    He wanted a constant, personal relationship

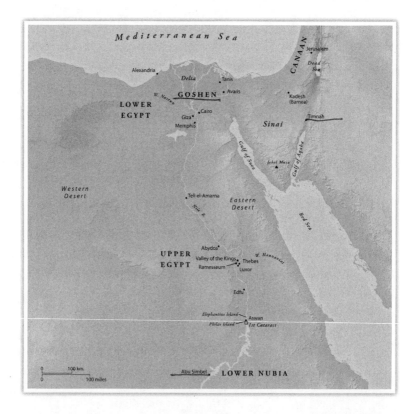

Small Group Bible Discovery and Discussion (22 minutes)

The Tabernacle: A Way to Remember Sinai

The centuries-long experience of God's people in Egypt — first as foreigners, then as slaves — had shaped the Hebrews into a people who still maintained aspects of their own religious culture but in other ways had become thoroughly immersed in the religious culture of Egypt. This is not in any way a statement of blame. After all, for four hundred years the Hebrews had been bombarded by Egypt's story that was played out in the rhythm of daily life along the Nile River and surrounded them in the portrayal of Egypt's deities and Pharaohs carved into the great monuments.

Certainly God would have to act with power and drama to gain the attention of the Hebrews and teach them how to live as his chosen people in the Promised Land. And he did! The plagues, the Passover, the crossing of the sea, miracles of water and manna as the Hebrews traveled toward Mount Sinai — all demonstrated the person and character of their God. And then they camped at Mount Sinai, the capstone experience of God's revelation of himself to them.

What would happen next? How would God's people know and remember him — not just on the journey to the Promised Land but forever? Let's see where the tabernacle fits into the story and consider how it was designed to be a sanctuary for God where his presence would live among his people as an ever-present reminder of his revelation at Mount Sinai.

1. God intended far more for his people than simply ending their suffering at the hands of the Egyptians. What did he say he would do for them, and how did he describe the future relationship he wanted with them? (See Exodus 6:6 – 8.)

   God is our Lord, He will deliver us, Free us, rescue us, redeem us. He wants us to be His people To be our God

2. During their time of bondage in Egypt, the Hebrew people became discouraged and in some ways lost sight of who their God was (Exodus 6:9). What did they discover about their God through the plagues, the Passover, their departure from Egypt, and their deliverance from Pharaoh's pursuing army at the sea? (See Exodus 14:30 – 15:18.)

What impact did their newly acquired knowledge of God have on their hearts?

What picture of hope and their future relationship with God do you see starting to form in the minds and hearts of the Hebrews?

3. After about forty days in the desert wilderness, where God had provided for them and protected them, the Israelites arrived at Mount Sinai. What was God's message and promise to them when they arrived at the mountain? (See Exodus 19:3 – 8.)

How did the people respond?

To what extent do you think they understood the kind of relationship God desired to have with them?

4. When God descended on Mount Sinai to meet with his people, it was an experience like no other! What were the physical and sensory manifestations of God's presence? (See Exodus 19:16 – 19; 20:18 – 21. You might want to list them!)

   How did the people respond to God's holy presence?

   How might this experience have influenced their faith and commitment to do "everything the Lord has said" (19:8)?

   What do you think it would have been like to have stood at the foot of the mountain with them?

5. How long do you think the experience of God's appearance at Mount Sinai impacted the faith commitment of the Israelites? (See Exodus 32:1.)

   In what ways does this help you understand God's command to build a sanctuary where his presence would live among his people always?

   How would the tabernacle and its design have helped the Hebrews remember their experiences at Mount Sinai?

Why do you think it would be important for God's people to be able to take the Sinai experience — the awe-filled memory of God's glory, the power of his presence, and the fire of an intimate relationship with the God of the universe — with them into the Promised Land?

THINK ABOUT IT

As a reminder, a sensory echo of the Mount Sinai experience, the tabernacle provided a way for the Israelites to take with them the memory of how God met them at his mountain in the desert. Consider the parallel characteristics of Mount Sinai and the tabernacle, each of which was a sanctuary for God's presence.

Mount Sinai	The Tabernacle
The people consecrated themselves and assembled at the foot of Mount Sinai. Limits were established to keep them from going up or even touching the mountain. The penalty for disobedience was death (Ex. 19:9–22).	The people could gather in the outer court where they could bring offerings to be made at the altar (Ex. 27:9–19).
At God's invitation, the priests, elders, and Moses went partway up the mountain to eat and drink in the presence of God (Ex. 24: 1–11).	Only Aaron and his fellow Levites were allowed to enter the holy place of the sanctuary to perform the duties God commanded. Anyone else was to be put to death (Num. 8:19–22; 18:1–7).
When the cloud of God's glory settled on Mount Sinai like a consuming fire, God called Moses to come up into the cloud to meet with him (Ex. 24:12–18).	In the holy of holies (Most Holy Place), a cloud of incense filled the space where the ark of the covenant was placed. Only Moses could enter and meet with God. Later, only the high priest could enter to fulfill his duties on the Day of Atonement (Lev. 16:1–2, 13, 29–34; Num. 7:89).

IN THIS ARTIST'S RENDERING OF GOD MEETING WITH HIS PEOPLE AT MOUNT SINAI, WE CAN ENVISION THE THREE LEVELS OF HOLINESS REPRESENTED: THE PEOPLE AT THE FOOT OF THE MOUNTAIN; THE PRIESTS, ELDERS, AND MOSES PARTWAY UP THE MOUNTAIN; AND MOSES ASCENDING INTO THE CLOUD AT THE SUMMIT.

Faith Lesson (6 minutes)

Shortly before the Israelites were finally to take possession of the Promised Land, Moses cautioned them to "watch yourselves closely so that you do not forget the things your eyes have seen or let them slip from your heart as long as you live" (Deuteronomy 4:9). For Israel, the tabernacle that God commanded them to build as a sanctuary for his presence was part of their watching and remembering. The tabernacle helped to keep alive in their hearts the fire of meeting God at Mount Sinai.

1. What do you think God wants his followers today to do with the powerful memories of their experience with him?

What makes it more difficult for you to do this? What makes it easier?

2. If you have had a profound experience of the presence of God in your life, in the life of someone you know, or in the life of your faith community, what was it like, and how did you respond?

In what way(s) did that experience give you a new sense of God's great power, holiness, and love?

What desires and responses did that experience inspire in your relationship with God?

What is your commitment to keep the memory of that experience alive in your heart, and how much work are you willing to put into taking the memory of that experience with you everywhere you go?

3. Which specific images, experiences, or words of the Bible help you to recognize God's presence in your life?

In what ways do these heighten your awareness of God and intimacy in your relationship with him?

Closing (1 minute)

Read Deuteronomy 4:9 – 10 aloud together: "Only be careful, and watch yourselves closely so that you do not forget the things your eyes have seen or let them slip from your heart as long as you live. Teach them to your children and to their children after them. Remember the day you stood before the LORD your God at Horeb, when he said to me, 'Assemble the people before me to hear my words so that they may learn to revere me as long as they live in the land and may teach them to their children.' "

Then pray, asking God to make you more aware of his presence with you always. Ask him to help you remember him, know him, and worship him with your whole heart every day of your life.

Memorize

> *Only be careful, and watch yourselves closely so that you do not forget the things your eyes have seen or let them slip from your heart as long as you live. Teach them to your children and to their children after them. Remember the day you stood before the LORD your God at Horeb, when he said to me, "Assemble the people before me to hear my words so that they may learn to revere me as long as they live in the land and may teach them to their children."*
>
> *Deuteronomy 4:9 – 10*

Learning to Live by the Word and Heart of God

In-Depth Personal Study Sessions

Day One | The Tabernacle: A Practice Rooted in Culture

The Very Words of God

> *Then the cloud covered the Tent of Meeting, and the glory of the LORD filled the tabernacle. Moses could not enter the Tent of Meeting because the cloud had settled upon it, and the glory of the LORD filled the tabernacle.*
>
> **Exodus 40:34–35**

Bible Discovery

Why God Chose a Tabernacle

God has always wanted to live in intimate relationship with his people and throughout history has worked to restore his presence with them. When the time came for him actually to live among his chosen people all the time, God communicated his desire to be with them through images and customs with which they already were familiar. He chose the visible, tangible symbol of the tabernacle, its furnishings, and its ritual to reveal his presence to his people.

Although we may need to devote some study to understanding God's desire as expressed through the tabernacle, it made perfect sense to the Israelites. God was communicating in a "language" they understood. Through the familiar metaphor of the tabernacle and the cultural practices that God reclaimed from pagan practices, the Israelites discovered how God was unlike all other gods they had known. They began to understand the relationship he desired to have with them.

1. What is the tabernacle called in Exodus 26:36?

Scholars have learned that as early as about 2000 BC Egyptian armies on the move would take a tent to use as a religious shrine. Also, the Hebrew word for "tent," *ohel*, that refers to the tabernacle in this passage, is believed to be an Egyptian word used to describe the tents of nomads. As you consider this historical and cultural background, what thoughts do you have about the way God chose to represent himself to his people during their journey to the Promised Land?

What connections do you think God may have wanted his people to make regarding their relationship with him and what he was accomplishing through them?

DID YOU KNOW?
A Long History of Tent Shrines

The relief of Ramses' war camp at the battle of Kadesh that is carved into the temple wall at Abu Simbel shows remarkable similarities to the design of the tabernacle. The basic structure comprises a two-chambered tent within a larger, rectangular, fenced enclosure that faces east. The smaller of the tent chambers is depicted as the throne room or residing place of the Pharaoh. Similar encampment and tent sanctuary designs are depicted in other Egyptian records.

continued on next page . . .

THIS CARVING OF RAMSES' WAR CAMP DEPICTED AT ABU SIMBEL IS SIMILAR TO RELIEFS DEPICTED AT OTHER EGYPTIAN TEMPLES. THE CAMP, SURROUNDED BY A FENCE OF ROUND-TOPPED LEATHER SHIELDS, IS ORIENTED TO THE EAST. INSIDE THE COMPOUND IS PHARAOH'S RECTANGULAR, TWO-CHAMBERED TENT. THE INNER CHAMBER, OR THRONE ROOM, PORTRAYS A WINGED IMAGE OF THE EGYPTIAN GOD HORUS ON EITHER SIDE OF THE PHARAOH'S CARTOUCHE.

THE TABERNACLE GOD INSTRUCTED THE ISRAELITES TO BUILD WAS ALSO AN ENCLOSED COURTYARD ORIENTED TO THE EAST. INSIDE, A RECTANGULAR, TWO-CHAMBERED TENT HOUSED THE INNER COURT AND THE HOLY OF HOLIES. WITHIN THE HOLY OF HOLIES, GOD'S PRESENCE RESIDED BETWEEN THE WINGED CHERUBIM ON THE COVER OF THE ARK OF THE COVENANT.

THE SHRINE AT TIMNAH AS IT APPEARS TODAY AND AN ARTIST'S RENDERING OF HOW ARCHAEOLOGISTS BELIEVE IT LOOKED WHEN IT WAS USED DURING ANCIENT TIMES

The tomb of Hetepheres (approximately 1600 BC), wife of Sneferu and mother of Cheops (the builder of the Great Pyramid), contained a gilded wood frame covered by curtains that was assembled much like the sanctuary.

continued on next page . . .

Tutankhamen's tomb (approximately 1350 BC) contained a shrine covered by linen cloth that was divided into two parts in a manner similar to that of the tabernacle.

The tent shrine to Hathor located at Timnah was originally built by Seti I (1318 – 1304 BC), but was intentionally destroyed by others. Egyptians repaired it but eventually abandoned it. More than a century later, the Midianites used it as a tent sanctuary for the worship of their gods.

To this day, some Bedouin nomads in the Middle East carry with them a tent-like structure made of thin boards with a tent on top. Fastened to the saddle of a camel, the structure represents the presence of Allah wherever it goes.

2. In addition to using a culturally familiar design for the tabernacle structure, God also incorporated other cultural icons into the tabernacle furnishings and rituals to help reveal himself and convey to his people the kind of relationship he desired to have with them. Consider some of these elements and how God reclaimed them from their traditional pagan use to communicate his message.

a. Ancient pagan worshipers made **sacrifices** of the finest foods in order to placate their gods so that the gods would view them with favor. Read Exodus 13:1, Leviticus 23:9 – 14, and Nehemiah 10:35, noting how God commanded his people to sacrifice to him. How is what God asked his people to do similar to and different from what pagan people believed their gods demanded?

What do you think God wanted to communicate through the sacrifices he required? (See Psalm 24:1; 1 Corinthians 10:26.)

b. Many ancient cultures had protective creatures, similar to **cherubim,** that possessed human, animal, or bird-like features and were often depicted in association with the gods. With what are cherubim identified in the Bible, and what do you think the cherubim sculpted on the cover of the ark of the covenant communicated about God to his people? (See Genesis 3:23 – 24; Exodus 25:17 – 22; Psalm 80:1; Revelation 4:2 – 11.)

c. In Egypt, priests conducted daily **incense** rituals intended to purify the image of the god and to persuade the god to enter the image. In contrast, what did incense provide in relationship to the presence of God? (See Leviticus 16:1 – 2, 12 – 13.)

d. In pagan belief, **idols** are representations of, or residing places for, the gods. As such, the idol is believed to take on the characteristics, abilities, persona, and power of the god it represents. Where did God say he would dwell if his people made a sanctuary for him? (See Exodus 25:8, 22.)

Did the sanctuary acquire any special power, or did God expect his people to worship it because his presence was there? Explain your answer.

What did God repeatedly teach his people about the worship of idols, and how does his presence in the tabernacle differ from what pagan people believed about idols and why they worshiped them? (See Exodus 20:3 – 6; 34:17; Deuteronomy 29:17 – 18; 32:21.)

e. The people of pagan cultures developed their own rituals regarding **access to the presence of their god(s)**. Who decided who was allowed to enter the holy of holies in the tabernacle where the presence of God lived, and under what conditions? (See Leviticus 16:1 – 2, 32 – 33.)

What do you think God was teaching his people through this requirement?

3. Early followers of Jesus also used cultural images and customs to explain God's message in a "language" their listeners would understand. In the first century AD, for example, the apostle Paul arrived in Athens to proclaim the message of Jesus to both Jews and Gentiles (Acts 17:16 – 33). What cultural icon did he use as a starting point for his message? (See Acts 17:23.)

What effect do you think Paul's use of an actual altar and inscription had on his listeners?

For how long do you think Paul's listeners would have been reminded of what he told them about their "unknown god" whenever they walked past that altar?

Reflection

Paul clearly communicated his method for revealing God to others in 1 Corinthians 9:19 – 23:

Though I am free and belong to no man, I make myself a slave to everyone, to win as many as possible. To the Jews I became like a Jew, to win the Jews. To those under the law I became like one under the law (though I myself am not under the law), so as to win those under the law. To those not having the law I became like one not having the law (though I am not free from God's law but am under Christ's law), so as to win those not having the law. To the weak I became weak, to win the weak. I have become all things to all men so that by all possible means I might save some. I do all this for the sake of the gospel, that I may share in its blessings.

What specific opportunities do you think Christians today have lost because we have failed to present the message of God and his restoring love in the language and cultural metaphors people understand? (List them.)

Identify several contemporary cultural experiences, images, or customs that you think would help people understand God's story as told in the Bible. For instance, what might you use to illustrate:

God's desire for relationship with individual people?

The reality of sin?

The true character of God?

The sacrificial love of Jesus?

The kind of life God desires his people to live?

In following Paul's example, who in your culture do you think you need to "become" like in order to better communicate God's story to people who do not know him?

What are the risks of adapting to the cultural icons rather than adapting the icons to God's message, and what can you do to guard against this?

What are the risks of misrepresenting God as you communicate through the icons of culture, and how will you keep his message pure?

Day Two | The Tabernacle: God Comes to Live Among His People

The Very Words of God

> *I will dwell among the Israelites and be their God. They will know that I am the* Lord *their God, who brought them out of Egypt so that I might dwell among them. I am the* Lord *their God.*

> **Exodus 29:45 – 46**

Bible Discovery

Getting to Know God in a New Way

When the Hebrews left Egypt, they were well acquainted with its gods. After all, the Hebrews had spent their entire lives surrounded by the stories of Egypt's pharaohs and deities portrayed on temples, tombs, and monuments. So when the God of the Hebrews took them out of Egypt and into the desert, how would they get to know him? They had heard that their God appeared to the patriarchs, and Moses told them that God had spoken to him, but how would *they* encounter their God? How would *they* come to know God's story and participate in his plan to reclaim his world? The tabernacle represented a new chapter in God's unfolding story — a significant change in how he revealed himself to his people.

1. Consider how God's people had encountered God's presence before the tabernacle was built. When and where had God made his presence known to individual people? (See Genesis 12:6 - 7; 28:10 - 17; Exodus 3:1 - 6; 19:3, 17 - 20.)

    Do you think most of the Hebrews expected God to appear to them? Why or why not?

2. While the Hebrews were still in Egypt, God began making himself known to them. From the miracles of the plagues to his protection and deliverance from Pharaoh's army at the Red Sea to his provision of manna, God's mighty acts demonstrated his love and desire for a relationship with his people. At Mount Sinai, God expressed to Moses the kind of relationship he desired to have with his people (Exodus 19:3 – 23:33).

    a. When Moses told the people everything God had said about how they were to live in relationship with him, how did they respond? (See Exodus 24:3.)

    b. What kind of a relationship did God then establish with them? (See Exodus 24:4 – 8.)

3. After the Israelites confirmed their relationship with God, what did he command them to build, and why? (See Exodus 25:8.)

    Had God ever lived among his people in this way previously?

    What was God's purpose for living among them, and how did this fit into his great plan to reclaim his world from the chaos of sin? (See Exodus 19:5 – 6; 29:45 – 46.)

The Israelites had come out of a culture where they lived in the midst of images of Egyptian gods. It was customary to appease and honor the Egyptian gods but not to have what could be called a "relationship" with them. What do you think the Israelites might have thought when they realized that their God actually wanted to live *with* them and be *known by* them?

PROFILE OF A PEOPLE
Cultures in Contrast

While Moses was up on Mount Sinai receiving from God the stone tablets of the covenant, the Israelites struggled to live by the word of God rather than by what they had "set their eyes on" in Egypt. Their doublemindedness led to a crisis in the camp (Exodus 32:1–3). Moses was focused on how they would build a sanctuary, a holy place where their invisible God could live with them so they could get to know him and his ways. At the same time, Aaron was making a golden calf so that the Israelites could focus on a visible god as they had done in Egypt. Consider the spiritual implications of the cultural contrasts between these two stories.

The Building of the Tabernacle	The Making of the Golden Calf
God's idea—Ex. 25:8–9; 29:45–46	Israelites' idea—Ex. 32:1–3
Made through willing offerings—Ex. 25:1–2	Made through demanded donations—Ex. 32:2–3
Well-planned, orderly process of painstaking, skilled construction—Ex. 25–31; 35–40	A hurried creation, resulting from impulsive action—Ex. 32:2–6
Priests ordained to serve and protect God's holiness—Ex. 29:1, 35–37, 44; Lev. 16:1–2	People offered sacrifices and then indulged in revelry—Ex. 32:6
Created a visible space among his people for an invisible God—Ex. 25:22	Created a visible image (idol)—Ex. 32:4

4. Getting to know God and learning to live by his word represented a significant — and difficult — change for his people. What had happened to the Hebrews while they were in Egypt that made them quick to go back to the familiar images and customs rather than responding to God with wholehearted obedience? (See Ezekiel 20:4 - 14.)

5. Where in the camp was the tabernacle always placed? (See Numbers 1:51 - 53; 2:1 - 2.)

    Why do you think God chose this location as the dwelling place for his presence?

    What do you think this location communicated to the Israelites?

6. What happened as soon as the tabernacle was finished and Moses set it up for the first time? (See Exodus 40:33 - 35.)

    What do you think the cloud of God's presence above the tabernacle communicated to the Israelites about their God and their relationship with him? (See Exodus 40:36 - 38.)

In what ways do you think the cloud of God's presence above the tabernacle was removing the influences of Egypt and training his people to trust and obey him so that they could fulfill their role in his ongoing story? (See Numbers 9:15 – 23.)

Reflection

The message of God's relationship with his people as revealed through the tabernacle metaphor isn't just for the Hebrews. It also speaks to God's people today. God's intent is, and has always been, to share an intimate relationship among or within his people. The tabernacle portrayed this desire and assured his people of his faithful presence.

Take time to read and meditate on the following portions of the Bible. Focus your thoughts against the background of the message God communicated to the Israelites through the tabernacle, where his presence lived among them. Consider how the message of God's desire to dwell among his people speaks to you.

> *Be strong and very courageous.... Do not let this Book of the Law depart from your mouth; meditate on it day and night, so that you may be careful to do everything written in it. Then you will be prosperous and successful. Have I not commanded you? Be strong and courageous. Do not be terrified; do not be discouraged, for the Lord your God will be with you wherever you go.*
>
> **Joshua 1:7 – 9**

> *The virgin will be with child and will give birth to a son, and they will call him Immanuel — which means, "God with us."*
>
> **Matthew 1:23**

> *Then the eleven disciples went to Galilee, to the mountain where Jesus had told them to go. When they saw him, they worshiped him; but some doubted. Then Jesus came to them and said, "All authority in heaven and on earth has been given to me. Therefore go and make disciples of all nations, baptizing them in the name of the Father and of the Son*

and of the Holy Spirit, and teaching them to obey everything I have commanded you. And surely I am with you always, to the very end of the age."

Matthew 28:16–20

When the day of Pentecost came, they were all together in one place. Suddenly a sound like the blowing of a violent wind came from heaven and filled the whole house where they were sitting. They saw what seemed to be tongues of fire that separated and came to rest on each of them. All of them were filled with the Holy Spirit and began to speak in other tongues as the Spirit enabled them.

Acts 2:1–4

Don't you know that you yourselves are God's temple and that God's Spirit lives in you? If anyone destroys God's temple, God will destroy him; for God's temple is sacred, and you are that temple.

1 Corinthians 3:16–17

Memorize

The cloud of the LORD was over the tabernacle by day, and fire was in the cloud by night, in the sight of all the house of Israel during all their travels.

Exodus 40:38

Day Three | God Calls His People to Build the Tabernacle

The Very Words of God

Then Moses summoned Bezalel and Oholiab and every skilled person to whom the LORD had given ability and who was willing to come and do the work. They received from Moses all the offerings the Israelites had brought to carry out the work of constructing the sanctuary.

Exodus 36:2–3

Bible Discovery

The Community Builds for God!

The tabernacle metaphor communicated an important message to the Israelites about the kind of relationship God wanted to have with them. In a cultural language they could understand, it helped them to realize the close, intimate relationship they could enjoy with their God. But the tabernacle experience wasn't only about the Israelites' relationship with God; it also was about their relationship with one another and their identity as a community of God's people. When Moses, as God commanded, told Israel to build the tabernacle, they learned about themselves — who they were and who they could become as a community united together to accomplish God's purpose.

1. Who did God say was to build his tabernacle (also "sanctuary") and its furnishings? (See Exodus 25:1 - 2, 8 - 10.)

   What is significant about God instructing "them" to build rather than instructing only Moses, or Bezalel, or Oholiab to build?

   What would be the effect of every Israelite having contributed to the building of God's dwelling place?

2. Building the tabernacle according to God's instructions was no small job! If you read all of God's instructions for the tabernacle (Exodus 25 – 30; also 36 – 39), you will be amazed by the work it required. For now, consider just a few examples of what the community of God's people made!

Object	Quantity	Size	Material	Other Features/ Details
Curtains (Ex. 26:1 – 6)				
Frame of the tabernacle (Ex. 26:15 – 29)				
Breastpiece (Ex. 28:15 – 28)				

Imagine! Fifty of this, twenty of that. Some items of hammered gold, others overlaid in bronze. Some made of fine linen, others of animal hides. Some framed in wood, others set with precious stones. Try to imagine the variety of skills and the number of people it took — working together — to complete this task. (Handling curtains that are approximately six by forty-two feet is not a job for one person!)

a. What do you think the community of God's people discovered about themselves and their God as they came together to accomplish this beautiful work?

b. In what ways might this experience have helped to turn a group of liberated slaves into a community of people who would live for God in the Promised Land?

3. God required that the sanctuary and its furnishings be made *exactly* as he instructed (Exodus 25:9). Why do you think it was important for God's people (who would soon enter the Promised Land to live in such a way that all the world would come to know their God) to learn to follow his instructions exactly?

4. Eventually the people completed the work and presented it to Moses. Exodus 39:32 – 43 describes their presentation of the finished tabernacle.

a. What was the result of their labor?

b. Imagine seeing all of the parts and furnishings of the tabernacle gathered together before Moses. What sense of accomplishment, connection with God, and unity of the community do you think the people felt that day?

c. What do you think God was impressing on the hearts of his people through this experience?

Reflection

The tabernacle in the desert has long since faded into the dust of history. Even the temple in Jerusalem no longer stands as the dwelling place of God. But God still lives within the hearts of his people, and he still desires to build up that community of obedient people who will continue his work of making him known to all the world.

Using the cultural language of the first century, Peter described the community of believers as those who, "also, like living stones, are being built into a spiritual house to be a holy priesthood, offering spiritual sacrifices acceptable to God through Jesus Christ" (1 Peter 2:5).

To what extent do you think God wants his people today to experience the sense of community unity and purpose

that the Israelites must have felt when Moses blessed them for their work on the tabernacle?

that Peter had in mind when he wrote of God's people being living stones in a spiritual house, a holy priesthood offering sacrifices?

Consider what binds a community of God's people together. Is it just sharing common interests or liking each other, or is it something deeper? If so, what is it?

If you ever have experienced being part of a strong community of faith, what made it work?

What work do you think God wants his community of people to join together in accomplishing today?

What do you think is essential in order for God's people to be successful in accomplishing this work as a unified community?

Memorize

So all the work on the tabernacle, the Tent of Meeting, was completed. The Israelites did everything just as the LORD commanded Moses.... Moses inspected the work and saw that they had done it just as the LORD had commanded. So Moses blessed them.

Exodus 39:32, 43

Day Four | The Tabernacle: Built from the Gifts of the People

The Very Words of God

The LORD said to Moses, "Tell the Israelites to bring me an offering. You are to receive the offering for me from each man whose heart prompts him to give."

Exodus 25:1 – 2

Bible Discovery

Giving Generously to the Work of the Lord

God commanded Moses to collect valuables from the people to be used in building the tabernacle. The response of God's people is truly amazing, particularly in light of how little they really had. Remember, the Israelites had just left Egypt for good, and they had done so in a hurry. They had no bank accounts, investments, or retirement funds. They had only the food, tools, household items, and valuables that they carried out of Egypt on foot! Would they give enough to accomplish the work God set before them?

1. While meeting with Moses on Mount Sinai, God said that he wanted his people to build a sanctuary for him. What specific thing did God ask the people do, and for what purpose? (See Exodus 25:1 – 2, 8.)

DID YOU KNOW?

The Hebrew word, *terumah*, translated in Exodus 25 as "offering," has a special meaning. It comes from a root word that means "to be exalted or lifted up" and refers to something that is set apart by its owner and dedicated to God's use.

Anything God's people freely give to him is lifted up for a higher purpose. In addition to offering material goods as *terumah*, God's people can lift up clean hands, a pure heart, their speech and voice, even their soul (Psalms 24:4; 25:1; 142:1).

2. Building the tabernacle as God's dwelling place was clearly an important part of God's unfolding story. We might think that God would command his people to give him gifts or use his authority to levy a tax in order to have the resources needed for the task. Instead, God asked for voluntary offerings. Why do you think God did this, especially since he assessed a payment to be used for maintaining the tabernacle later (Exodus 30:11 – 16)?

What do you think the opportunity, rather than obligation, to give to the Lord said to the Israelites about the kind of relationship God desired to have with them?

What do you think it said about the kind of people he wanted them to be?

3. List the specific items God asked the people to bring as offerings. (See Exodus 25:3 – 7.)

   Which items, and how large a quantity of them, do you think people who had been slaves would, or would not, have had?

   How had the Israelites obtained their more valuable possessions? (See Exodus 3:21 – 22; 11:2 – 3; 12:33 – 36.)

   What indicates that these possessions were gifts from God? (See Genesis 15:12 – 14.)

4. When Moses finished telling the Israelites what God had said about offerings to build the tabernacle, how did the people respond? (See Exodus 35:20 – 29; 36:2 – 7.)

Reflection

And the people continued to bring freewill offerings morning after morning.... Then Moses gave an order and they sent this word throughout the camp: 'No man or woman is to make anything else as an offering for the sanctuary. And so the people were restrained from bringing more, because what they already had was more than enough to do all the work.

Exodus 36:3 – 7

Just imagine the scene — the whole community abundantly giving and joyfully working together to complete the work! Even though they were totally dependent on God to provide for their needs, they gave until Moses made them stop!

Is this the response you would have expected from them? Why or why not?

What do you think this response meant to God, and to the people themselves?

What do you think it would have meant to your walk of faith to have participated in such an experience?

In a sense, the offerings the Israelites gave were their "bank account" for starting a new life in the Promised Land. So what God had asked his people to give was a sacrifice.

Why do you think God asked so much from people who had so little? (Remember, there were no moving vans for the Israelites. They were carrying everything they owned.)

How important do you think it is for God's people today to willingly make similar sacrifices in order to participate in the work God is doing?

Which of your possessions or which aspects of your lifestyle are you willing to sacrifice to God?

What would be difficult about making that sacrifice?

How much would you have to trust God in order to do it?

Memorize

Then the whole Israelite community withdrew from Moses' presence, and everyone who was willing and whose heart moved him came and brought an offering to the LORD for the work on the Tent of Meeting, for all its service, and for the sacred garments.... And so the people were restrained from bringing more, because what they already had was more than enough to do all the work.

Exodus 35:20–21; 36:6–7

Day Five | God Uses the Skill of His People

The Very Words of God

All who are skilled among you are to come and make everything the LORD has commanded.

Exodus 35:10

Bible Discovery

Qualified to Build God's Sanctuary

Building the tabernacle required the skills of the whole community
of God's people. Some tasks required people who could spin, weave,
and embroider in linen, goat hair, and gold. Other tasks required
people to cut and set precious stones or to construct furnishings
of wood and fine metalwork. Still other tasks required people who
could build wood beams and posts or had the skill of a perfumer.
And all of these tasks demanded workers with the wisdom to do the
work exactly as God instructed.

1. What kinds of skills were needed to complete the work of
    the tabernacle, and how had the men and women of Israel
    acquired those skills? (See Exodus 28:3; 31:1 - 11; 35:25 - 26.)

2. On which two men did God choose to bestow special abili-
    ties that were necessary for accomplishing the work of the
    tabernacle? (See Exodus 31:1 - 6; 35:30 - 36:1.)

    List the special qualifications God had given to Bezalel.

    List the special qualifications God had given to Oholiab.

    Which do you think were the most important skills or quali-
    fications that God gave to these men, and why?

3. As is often the case in exploring the account of God's story played out in history, knowing something of the language, customs, or lifestyle of the people involved can give us valuable insight into the meaning and message of the Bible. Consider, for example, the two men God singled out for leadership in building the tabernacle: Bezalel and Oholiab.

   a. Which tribes were each of these men from? (See Exodus 31:1 – 6.)

   b. What were the responsibilities of their respective tribes during Israel's time in the desert? (See Numbers 10:11 – 14, 25.)

   c. When God chose men from both the leading tribe of Israel and the rear-guard tribe, what do you think he was saying about the community nature of the task he was calling his people to do?

   d. The name *Bezalel* means "in the shadow (protection) of God" and the name *Oholiab* means "the tent of the father," which implies being under the protection of the father. What insights do the meanings of these names provide regarding the important nature of their work in building the tabernacle?

    e. What were these men responsible for protecting? (See Exodus 25:9.)

Reflection

It is unusual to find in one person the combination of skills that Bezalel and Oholiab each possessed. God truly did "fill" them with the abilities necessary to accomplish the task he assigned to them. But God also filled Bezalel from the tribe of Judah "with the Spirit of God" (Exodus 31:3, 35:30 – 31).

Why do you think God gave his Spirit (literally a "divine spirit of wisdom") to equip Bezalel for the job?

What challenges do you think Bezalel faced in leading God's people to build the tabernacle according to God's plan and standards?

What do you think would have happened if Bezalel had been lax in protecting God's plan and in meeting God's standards for the tabernacle? What if he had allowed the Israelites to change the requirements for building the tabernacle because they had other preferences or wanted to make the job easier?

There is a sense in which all of God's people are like Bezalel and Oholiab — called to build the community in which God's presence will dwell.

With which abilities has God gifted you for this task, and to what extent are you using them for that purpose?

When have you been lax in using your abilities exactly according to God's instructions or standards, and what has been the result?

In what ways do you need the wisdom of God's Spirit to help you live in such a way that you create a sanctuary — a place — for God's presence to dwell in your life? Your family? Your faith community? Your world?

MAKING SPACE FOR GOD

If God had led them by the shortest route, the Hebrews could have reached Canaan, the land God had promised to give them, just a few weeks after leaving Egypt. Instead, they traveled through the desert for about forty days before arriving at Mount Sinai. They camped at the foot of the mountain for another forty days while God gave Moses the Ten Commandments (Hebrew, "tablets of the Ten Words") and the rest of the Torah. Then God commanded the Israelites to construct the tabernacle, the sanctuary where his presence would live among them. Preparing the tabernacle took approximately nine months! It was erected for the first time on the anniversary of their departure from Egypt, the first day of their new calendar year.

Why the delays? Why did God dedicate so much time and effort to these activities? Couldn't he have waited to give the Torah in the Promised Land? The people had already followed the cloud of his presence to Mount Sinai, so why build a sanctuary? We may never know the answers to these questions because we cannot know the mind of God. However, we can conclude that the way the exodus unfolded, the events at Mount Sinai, and the building of the tabernacle were extremely important to God. And he wanted them to be significant in the lives of his people as well.

Consider, for example, that nearly fifty chapters of the Torah are devoted to the tabernacle! God's instructions for the tabernacle begin in Exodus 25, are repeated in Exodus 35, and continue until Exodus 40. All of Leviticus, which God gave to Moses on Mount Sinai, relates to tabernacle rituals. The chapters relating to the tabernacle's construction and ritual include detailed instructions concerning each piece of furniture and the raw materials that were to be used. Additional chapters in Numbers describe how the Israelites were to pack up, carry, and reassemble the tabernacle when they traveled. In contrast, only two chapters — Genesis 1 - 2 — are devoted to God's creation of the entire universe!

Perhaps the fact that the exodus was a journey from slavery to worship (in Hebrew, from *avodah* to *avodah* since the same word is translated both as *work/slavery* and as *worship*) helps us to understand why the tabernacle was so significant to God. The use of the word *avodah* highlights the effort God expected his people to expend in worshiping him. Every part of the tabernacle and its function conveyed spiritual meaning that served to remind God's people of the significance of their relationship with him in everyday life. Perhaps it was important because in Egypt God's people had been surrounded by hundreds of gods displayed in relief and statue, and even had small idols to carry and keep in their homes. In the most holy place of the tabernacle, the presence of the unseen God of the Israelites, for whom no idols were to be made, would actually live among them (Exodus 25:8)!

Although it is not possible, in this brief study, to fully explore all that God wanted to teach the Israelites concerning the tabernacle, various aspects of its construction apply to his people at all times and in all places — including people today! God desired for his people to be his partners in "making space" for him in their lives, so he provided the exact, detailed pattern for his sanctuary, and his people donated the building materials and constructed it. God also wanted his people to not only remember the incredible depictions of his glory at Mount Sinai but to experience every day the awe and fire of his presence with them. Let's see what we can learn about how God's people can make space for God in their lives.

Opening Thoughts (3 minutes)

The Very Words of God

> *I will consecrate the Tent of Meeting and the altar and will consecrate
> Aaron and his sons to serve me as priests. Then I will dwell among the
> Israelites and be their God. They will know that I am the LORD their
> God, who brought them out of Egypt so that I might dwell among them.
> I am the LORD their God.*

Exodus 29:44 – 46

Think About It

To some extent we experience life according to what is most important to us. For instance, if we are consumed by our own needs and
don't "make room" in our lives for showing compassion, we may not
notice the needs of suffering people whose paths we cross every
day. We may become blind to the homeless or the empty stares of
hungry children.

Can you share any examples of what you have learned to see more
clearly because of the values that are most important to you? Or, in
what ways do you see life differently when you are more focused
on your relationship with God than when you are neglecting that
relationship?

DVD Notes (32 minutes)

How to keep the "fire" of Sinai burning

The parts of the tabernacle—a "portable Sinai"

The place where God lived

The "bigger picture" of the tabernacle:

Dealing with sin

An intimate place to meet God

A new creation—"God's people make the space; God will fill it!"

Have we created space for God today?

DVD Discussion (6 minutes)

1. Study the map on page 62 showing Canaan (Israel) and the Sinai Peninsula. How far is it from the region of the traditional Mount Sinai (Jebel Musa) to Kadesh Barnea, the location from which the Israelites would send spies into Canaan?

   With their long-awaited destination so close, how important must the tabernacle have been to God for him to have the Israelites spend most of a year constructing it before proceeding on their journey?

   How might what God wanted this delay to accomplish in the lives and hearts of his people compare to what he wanted to accomplish by leading them into the desert rather than straight into Canaan via "The Way of the Philistines" (along the Mediterranean Sea) when they first left Egypt (Exodus 13:17)?

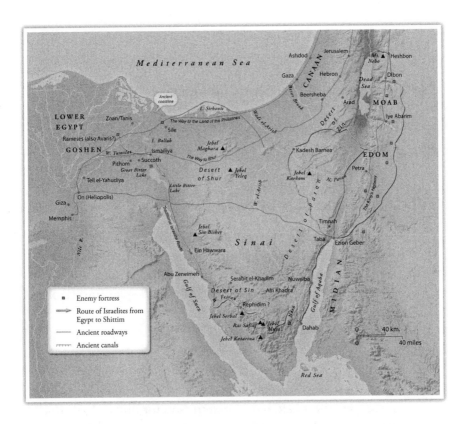

2. When you first saw the replica of the tabernacle, what impressed you? Surprised you?

How does it compare to your previous image or understanding of the tabernacle?

In what ways did seeing a visual replica of the tabernacle add to or change your image and understanding of God?

3. As you learned about the different parts and furnishings of the tabernacle, what new insight did you gain into how God wanted the Israelites to experience and worship him?

4. In what ways does having a visual picture of the tabernacle and its role in the life of the Israelites help you to better understand your faith and keep it alive in your heart and life?

For example, what did you think when the scapegoat ritual and its connection to Jesus was explained?

Small Group Bible Discovery and Discussion (13 minutes)

"Making Space" for God's Presence

When God commanded Moses to have the Israelites make a "sanctuary" where he would live *among* them (Exodus 25:8), the entire community got involved. Try to imagine the awe, joy, and intimate connection they felt as they built and formed the place where God's presence would live! What if you had embroidered the curtains of the sanctuary, hammered the lampstand into shape, or shaped the wood for the ark of the covenant? Can you begin to imagine the intimate connection you would have felt every time you looked up to see the cloud of God's presence above the sanctuary that you helped to build? Unlike the gods the Hebrews had known in Egypt, the living God of Israel could speak and desired to be in such close relationship with his people that he would live among them — in their camp — in the space that they made for him.

1. Before sin entered the picture, God and the people he had created enjoyed close companionship in the Garden of Eden (Genesis 2:15 – 23; 3:8 – 9). As part of God's plan to redeem humankind from the sin that had destroyed that relationship, what did he intend to do in and through his chosen people, the Israelites? (See Exodus 19:2 – 6.)

2. In what ways did God respond when his people — his treasured possession — obeyed him and created space for him in their lives:

   a. At Mount Sinai, when the Israelites consecrated themselves? (See Exodus 19:10 – 11, 14 – 19; 20:18 – 19; Deuteronomy 5:22 – 26.)

b. After the Israelites completed the tabernacle — in effect making a holy "space" for their God to live among them? (See Leviticus 9:22 – 24; Exodus 40:33 – 38.)

c. After the temple in Jerusalem was completed? (See 1 Kings 6:11 – 13; 8:6 – 11.)

d. What do these examples reveal to you about the intensity of God's desire to live *among* and *within* his people?

THE TABERNACLE: GOD'S DWELLING PLACE AMONG HIS PEOPLE

POINT TO PONDER
A Wonderful Paradox

How can a holy and majestic God, who is present everywhere, live in a tent or temple (Exodus 40:34–35; 1 Kings 8:10–11, 22–30; Psalm 139:3–12; Isaiah 66:1–2; Jeremiah 23:23–24; Acts 17:24)? Our finite minds cannot comprehend the great paradox of the completely transcendent God living among and within his people, yet the tabernacle taught both truths. God is unseen and ever present, and we, his created beings, are unworthy to enter his holy presence. But God chose to be present with the ancient Israelites and live between the cherubim on the ark of the covenant in the holy of holies in the tabernacle!

3. How does God's presence among his people set them apart from all others, and what message does it convey to other nations? (See Deuteronomy 4:7.)

   Do you think God's desire to live among his people is any less today than it has been in the past? Why or why not?

   When God's presence is evident in the midst of his people today, to what extent do you think other people notice, and what impact does it have?

FOR GREATER UNDERSTANDING
God's Dwelling Place

One of the biblical terms used for the tabernacle is "tent" (Hebrew: *ohel,* as in Exodus 26:36) or "tent of meeting" (Exodus 29:42). Jewish thought reminds us that God wanted to be with his people, in a beautiful tent, as they traveled through the desert. The term *tent* stresses the portable nature of God's presence that moved with the Israelites from place to place. In contrast, the gods of the surrounding pagan nations were local and had no power over where they lived. So it was important for God's people to learn that their God would be with them wherever they went.

God's dwelling place among his people also conveyed a deeper spiritual significance. In Hebrew, the phrase "dwell *among* them" (Exodus 25:8, italics added) can also read, "dwell *within* them." The tabernacle was not only to be the focal point of God's presence in the Israelites' camp, but its courts, rooms, furnishings, and practices were designed to open the hearts of the people to the holy Creator God they worshiped so that he would dwell within *them.* In a sense, the presence of God was with the Israelites not only in the tabernacle but because of it, and they could share that presence with their world as if they also were God's tabernacle or sanctuary (Psalm 114:1 – 2). The tabernacle was to portray what the Israelites were to be to all nations — the very place where God's presence could be found!

In a similar way, John 1:1 – 2, 14 reveals how God later manifested his presence through his Son, Jesus the Messiah, who came and "made his dwelling among us." The Greek translation of John 1:14 literally reads "pitched his tent" or "set up his tabernacle" among us. Just think of the ways by which the ancient tabernacle provided a picture of what God would do through Jesus!

And God had in store something even more amazing! After Jesus died, lived again, and ascended into heaven, God displayed his presence within his people in an even more profound way. At that time, God's presence lived in the temple in Jerusalem. God's people, and people from other nations who desired to know him, traveled to the temple to worship him. But on

continued on next page . . .

Pentecost, as Jesus' followers gathered near the temple, God's Spirit came to rest on them — making them his dwelling place, his sanctuary, for all the world to see (Acts 2:1 – 4; 1 Corinthians 3:16 – 17; Ephesians 2:19 – 22).

Today, thousands of years after the tabernacle was built, God's dwelling place is still portable. God's presence is within every person who has a relationship with him through Jesus. Wherever that person goes, he or she literally brings God's presence and is to demonstrate that presence to a watching world.

Faith Lesson (5 minutes)

When they constructed the tabernacle, the Israelites "made space" for God, and he came to live among them. Filled with awe that their God — unlike any gods they had known in Egypt — would actually *live* among them, they rejoiced in his presence and because of his presence. But it can be difficult for us to comprehend the significance of God's move to dwell among his people — the ancient Israelites as well as his people who are living today. So the lessons of the tabernacle remain highly relevant.

1. How important is it for you to know God — to not only know about him, but to experience his indwelling presence in your life — to be with God, to be near him, to know him as your Lord?

2. In what way(s) has seeing the video about the tabernacle changed your understanding of how much God wants to dwell in and be involved in the lives of his people?

In what way(s) has your understanding of God's desire to dwell in *your* life changed?

In what ways do you need to "make space" for God to dwell within you?

3. If you follow Jesus, there is a sense in which you are his "portable tabernacle" who brings his presence everywhere you go. In what ways does this realization affect your thoughts, words, desires, and actions?

Closing (1 minute)

Read Exodus 29:45 – 46 aloud together: "Then I will dwell among the Israelites and be their God. They will know that I am the LORD their God, who brought them out of Egypt so that I might dwell among them. I am the LORD their God."

Then pray and invite the living God to make his presence at home within you. Ask him to forgive you for your sins, to make you pure and holy before him. Ask him to fill you with his presence so that you will display his true nature to people wherever you go.

Memorize

Then I will dwell among the Israelites and be their God. They will know that I am the LORD their God, who brought them out of Egypt so that I might dwell among them. I am the LORD their God.

Exodus 29:45 – 46

Learning to Live by the Word and Heart of God

In-Depth Personal Study Sessions

Day One | A Closer Look at the Tabernacle

The Very Words of God

> So the tabernacle was set up on the first day of the first month in the
> second year.... Then the cloud covered the Tent of Meeting, and the
> glory of the LORD filled the tabernacle. Moses could not enter the Tent of
> Meeting because the cloud had settled upon it, and the glory of the LORD
> filled the tabernacle.
>
> Exodus 40:17, 34–35

Bible Discovery

The "Rooms" and "Furnishings" in God's Dwelling Place

We cannot fully comprehend that the all-powerful, transcendent
Creator God instructed the Israelites to build the place for his presence to dwell among them. But if we study what God had his people
build, how they built it, and why, we will gain a deeper understanding of our awesome, faithful, and loving God! This is because the
tabernacle was more than a suitable place for God's holy presence.
The tabernacle, its furnishings, and its ritual are also a metaphor for
God's relationship with his people!

1. *The Courtyard.* The tabernacle (tent) that housed the holy
    place and most holy place was surrounded by a rectangular
    courtyard measuring one hundred cubits (150 feet) east to
    west and fifty cubits (75 feet) north to south.[1] The court-
    yard was enclosed by white linen curtains that separated
    the sacred (holy) areas inside from the profane (fallen) areas
    outside. The linen curtains were five cubits (7.5 feet) high
    and were attached by silver hooks to acacia wood pillars
    set in bronze bases. On the east side, the curtain extended

**THE OUTER COURTYARD OF THE TABERNACLE, SHOWING THE ALTAR
AND BRONZE LAVER, AND THE SANCTUARY**

from the corners toward the center for fifteen cubits (22.5 feet), leaving an opening of twenty cubits (30 feet). A screen of colorfully embroidered (blue, purple, and crimson) linen hung from four pillars and closed this opening. The only entrance to the courtyard was by the curtained gate (Exodus 27:9 – 18; Numbers 3:26), which represented God's invitation to his people to move from the fallen world outside to find forgiveness and refuge inside.

According to the following Scripture texts, which prominent items were located in the courtyard, and what was their function in the relationship between God and his people?

Exodus 20:24 – 26; 27:1 – 8.

Exodus 30:17 – 21

2. *The tabernacle (sanctuary or tent of meeting).* This tent
   was enclosed on three sides by ten curtains of violet, purple,
   and scarlet fabric into which figures of cherubim were
   embroidered. Each curtain was about forty-two feet long
   and six feet wide and was placed over a supportive wooden
   structure to form the walls and roof of the tabernacle. The
   eastern side of the tabernacle (facing the laver and altar)
   was open for entry and "closed" with another embroidered
   curtain suspended from five gold-plated pillars set in bronze
   bases. Eleven curtains of goat hair covered the entire inner
   "tent," including its sides, so that no inner curtains could be
   seen from the outside. Two additional layers of animal skin
   covered the outside of the structure.

a. What details does the Bible provide concerning the "furnishings" that God instructed Moses to have the Israelites build for the holy place, and what was their function in the relationship between God and his people?

Text	Description and Function of the Furnishing	Did You Know?
Ex. 25:23–30; Lev. 24:5–9		The table of the consecrated bread of the presence held twelve loaves of bread (representing the twelve tribes) that were not touched until Sabbath, when the priests ate them.
Ex. 25:31–40; Lev. 24:1–4; Num. 8:4		The menorah or lampstand, for which no size is specified, was fashioned from a single block of gold, not overlaid like other furnishings. Scholars have noted Egyptian influence in its description, such as its shaft that appears to be like a "reed" that flourished along the Nile (Ex. 2:1–3). The word translated "cups" (Ex. 25:33) probably came from an Egyptian word too. These connections support the tradition that the menorah had a unique role in helping the Hebrews to understand their God and distinguish him from the idols of Egypt.
Ex. 30:1–6; 37:25–29; Lev. 16:1–2, 12–13		The incense offered in the tabernacle is believed to be a metaphorical reminder of God's constant presence as symbolized by the pillar of fire and cloud (Ex. 13:21–22). The appearance of the cloud of incense came after the tabernacle was completed and indicated God's satisfaction in its construction. Later text (Ps. 141:1–2; Rev. 8:3–5) reveals that the prayers of God's people are like incense—a sweet smell to God.

b. The veil—a dividing curtain made of the same material and embroidered in the same way as the inner curtains—separated the holy place (about 30 x 15 x 15 feet) from the most holy place (holy of holies; about 15 x 15 x 15 feet). What details does the Bible provide concerning the "furnishing" that God instructed Moses to have the Israelites build for the most holy place, and what was its function in the relationship between God and his people?

Text	Description and Function of the Piece	Did You Know?
Ex. 25:10–22; Lev. 16:15–17		The ark of the covenant, the most sacred object in the most sacred place, contained the tablets of the Ten Commandments. It was the first item God described when issuing instructions for building the tabernacle. On the ark rested a slab of gold called the "atonement cover." Rising out of this cover as part of it, one from each end, were two cherubim that faced the center, their wings extended over it. This covered space, thought of as God's throne, was where God's presence lived.

3. After all parts of the tabernacle were completed exactly as God had commanded, who set up the tabernacle and what happened as soon as the work was complete? (See Exodus 39:42 – 40:35.)

Reflection

Think of all the effort the Israelites put into "making space for God." It took nearly a year to complete the tabernacle, which included the beautifully embroidered curtains, the bronze altar, the lampstand, the ark of the covenant, and other furnishings. Then God came to his people again, as he had at Mount Sinai, and *lived* among them! His move into the tabernacle had significant implications for his relationship with the Israelites and for his people today.

Consider, for example, the many times Moses met with God at Mount Sinai. (See Exodus 3:1 – 4; 19:3 – 4, 16 – 20, just to name a few.) Where did God speak to Moses after the tabernacle was completed? (See Exodus 25:22; Leviticus 1:1; Numbers 1:1; 7:89; Deuteronomy 31:14 – 16.)

What does the fact that Moses never again climbed Mount Sinai to speak with God after the tabernacle was completed communicate to you about the importance of the tabernacle in God's relationship with his people?

Consider, too, the language used to describe the tabernacle. The Hebrew word often translated "sanctuary" (Exodus 25:8) is *mikdash* (derived from the Hebrew *kadosh*:"holy") and implies a place, dwelling, or resting place that is devoted entirely to the sacred. The sanctuary (tabernacle) was sacred not because the space itself was holy, but because God's unapproachable and holy presence resided there. If you are a follower of Jesus, what are the implications of the holiness of the tabernacle for your life, which is God's visible "tabernacle" in your world?

The term *mishkan*, the most common Hebrew word translated "tabernacle," is used ninety-four times in the Torah and comes from the root *shakan* ("to settle" or "to live with"). The Hebrew word translated "neighbor," *shaken*, comes from the same root. So *mishkan* emphasizes God's nearness and closeness, and implies that God came to the tabernacle in order to be near his people like a neighbor! If you are a follower of Jesus, what are the implications of God's desire to live in relationship near you?

In what sense do you think the way in which God chose to be present among his people in the tabernacle was a significant step toward what God's people can experience today?

To what extent are you experiencing that kind of relationship with God?

Which insights into God's relationship with his people through the tabernacle have helped you to gain a better understanding of your relationship with him, and how will your relationship be different from now on?

Day Two | The Tabernacle as a Wedding Chamber

The Very Words of God

> *I remember the devotion of your youth, how as a bride you loved me and followed me through the desert, through a land not sown.*
>
> **Jeremiah 2:2**

Bible Discovery

God Comes to Live with His Bride

A careful study of the Bible reveals the amazing truth that God the Creator desires to establish a loving, intimate relationship with his people. And according to the Jewish understanding, what happened at Mount Sinai was a "wedding" between God and his bride, the people of Israel. That experience not only shaped the Israelites' relationship with God, but was part of his plan to redeem his world from sin and restore *shalom* — order, purpose, harmony. The Bible, in fact, uses word pictures of marriage to describe the Israelites' Sinai experience. It portrays God as a faithful husband who desired a personal and deep relationship with his bride. The tabernacle was essential to that picture. It provided the holy, pure place where God could live in intimate relationship with his people.

1. What amazing word picture concerning his people did God use (Jeremiah 2:2) to describe the weeks of travel through the desert between his rescue of the Hebrews from Egypt and their arrival at Mount Sinai?

What had God done to express his love for his people, and what did he desire them to be? (See Exodus 19:3 – 6; Deuteronomy 7:6 – 9, 12.)

Although he had already demonstrated the kind of husband he was by his patience, provision, and protection of his people, what did God give them at Mount Sinai that summarized how much he loved them and detailed how his people were to express their love for him? (See Exodus 20:1 – 17; 31:12 – 18; see also Deuteronomy 4:5 – 14; 6:4 – 9; 7:9.)

FOR GREATER UNDERSTANDING
The Wedding Images of Sinai

The Hebrew word *laqakh* describes the action of taking a wife for oneself, or taking a wife for another person. God often used this word to describe his relationship with Israel. The word is used in Exodus 6:6 – 8, which records God's promises to redeem the Hebrew slaves and "take" them as his "own people" and be their God.

In a manner similar to a Jewish bride who prepares herself by taking a ritual bath (*mikveh*) the day before her wedding, God instructed the Hebrews to purify and consecrate themselves in preparation for their meeting with him at Mount Sinai (Exodus 19:9 – 15, 20 – 24).

On the appointed day, the Israelites — God's "bride" — stood at the foot of the mountain as the presence of their holy God descended on Mount Sinai in a covering of smoke, darkness, lightning, and thunder and spoke to them (Exodus 19:17). The Hebrew word translated as "stood" also implies being "under" or "beneath." So the Israelites can be thought of as not just standing at the base of the mountain but standing under God's great *chuppah*, the canopy under which the bride and groom stand in a traditional Jewish wedding. To be under God's *chuppah* is to be covered with the canopy of his intimate, protective love.

During ancient times, covenants formally defined and carefully spelled out the mutually agreed upon commitments and responsibilities of many kinds of relationships, including the marriage relationship. Summary tablets (such as the Ten Commandments) representing the total relationship between the parties were also provided. Today, traditional Jewish weddings echo this ancient practice when a *ketubah* or "marriage contract" is read while the bride is under the *chuppah*. Although no one would argue that the Ten Commandments were a formal *ketubah* between God and his people, they could be viewed in this light. In keeping with the biblical marriage metaphor of the Israelites being God's bride, the commandments summarize God's ten vows or guidelines for a good marriage.

After the Israelites received the Torah, Moses wrote down every word that God had revealed on Mount Sinai. Then he built an altar, set up twelve stones representing Israel's twelve tribes, and offered burnt offerings and fellowship offerings of young bulls. Then he sprinkled half the covenant blood on the altar and, after reading the Book of the Covenant, sprinkled the other half of the covenant blood on the people. These actions symbolized that God had purified his people, sealed (ratified) their (marriage) covenant, and established fellowship (relationship) with them.

NOTE: An in-depth exploration of the "marriage" imagery displayed by God's interaction with his people at Mount Sinai can be found in *Faith Lessons vol. 9: Fire on the Mountain* (Session 5, "Led You Like a Bride: A Wedding at Sinai").

2.   What do you learn about the nature of God's desired relationship with his people from the use of the marriage metaphor in the following passages, and what do these examples reveal to you about the nature of the relationship God wants *you* to experience with him?

   Isaiah 54:5

   Jeremiah 31:31 – 32

   Hosea 2:14 – 20

3.   In the culture of ancient Israel, the physical union of a newly married couple was a holy, sacramental moment of two people becoming one, and it occurred in a literal bridal chamber (*chuppah*). After God entered an eternal, covenantal relationship with his people at Mount Sinai, he told them to build a tabernacle where he would *dwell* among them — not just to exist there, but to have a place to experience an intimate relationship with them. In what holy place did God meet with his people? (See Exodus 25:22; 29:42 – 45; 30:6, 34 – 36.)

   In light of your understanding of the tabernacle, in what ways was it like a bridal chamber?

In what ways did it symbolize and nurture the Hebrews' growing, intimate relationship with their God, who loved them as his bride?

4. During ancient times, when two parties made a covenant they each typically placed a summary copy of that contract in a most sacred place. It is Jewish tradition for a married couple to place their *ketubah* — the marriage contract specifying the commitments they have made to one another — in the sanctuary of their bedroom. What is significant about where the Ten Commandments — the summary document of the covenant between God and his people — was to be placed? What does it suggest about the role of the tabernacle in God's relationship with his people? (See Exodus 25:10 – 22; Deuteronomy 10:1 – 5.)

5. What powerful metaphors in Revelation 19:6 – 9 describe the moment when Jesus — the sinless Lamb of God — returns to the faithful community of Christ followers?

Reflection

It may feel a little strange for us to think about God and his people in terms of the word picture of a bridegroom and bride. Yet that relationship is closest to how God wanted to express his love for his people. God chose his "unwanted" bride and took her out of Egypt. He courted her and brought her to himself at Mount Sinai. Then he had his people make a sacred place where that relationship could be expressed and grow. God led his people through these experiences because he wanted them, as his bride, to experience the full depth of his love for them.

For a moment, put yourself in the place of the Israelites. How do you think the tabernacle would add to your knowledge (experience) of God's love for you and nurture a deeper, more intimate and faithful relationship with him?

In what ways does your knowledge of the tabernacle help you to understand the depth of God's love for you today?

To what extent does it rekindle your desire to experience a more intimate, personal relationship with God?

In what way(s) do the images of the relationship between God and the Israelites, his bride, refresh your love for God and inspire delight in your relationship with him?

What in your life is (or could be) a type of tabernacle or sanctuary where you experience your relationship with God on an intimate level?

Memorize

For your Maker is your husband — the LORD Almighty is his name — the Holy One of Israel is your Redeemer; he is called the God of all the earth.

Isaiah 54:5

Day Three | The Scapegoat: A Foreshadowing of the Messiah

The Very Words of God

> *When Aaron has finished making atonement for the Most Holy Place, the Tent of Meeting and the altar, he shall bring forward the live goat. He is to lay both hands on the head of the live goat and confess over it all the wickedness and rebellion of the Israelites — all their sins — and put them on the goat's head. He shall send the goat away into the desert in the care of a man appointed for the task. The goat will carry on itself all their sins to a solitary place; and the man shall release it in the desert.*
>
> *Leviticus 16:20 – 22*

Bible Discovery

In a Manner Like the Scapegoat, Jesus Took Our Sins on Himself

Regular sacrifices on the altar of the tabernacle played a significant role in the Hebrews' spiritual lives. Guilt offerings, burnt offerings, and sin offerings all involved the sacrifice of animals. But the annual sacrifice on the Day of Atonement stood out as a picture of God's forgiveness of his people's sins. On that day only, the high priest was allowed to enter the holy of holies to sprinkle blood on the atonement cover as part of the ritual for cleansing from sin. Then, the high priest would lay his hands on a live goat, symbolically placing the sins of all of Israel on its head, and send it out of the camp and into the desert. As strange as this ritual may seem to us, it foreshadowed the sacrificial death of Jesus, who took the sins of the whole world on himself.

1. Instructions for the Day of Atonement, the Israelites' annual atonement and cleansing ritual, are found in Leviticus 16:2 – 31.

    a. What steps did the high priest (in this case, Aaron, Moses' brother) have to do before entering the tabernacle to conduct the sacrificial ritual on the Day of Atonement? (See vv. 3 – 13.)

    b.   What protected the high priest from death when he entered the most holy place? (See vv. 12 – 13.)

    c.   What did the high priest do in the holy of holies, and why? (See vv. 14 – 17.)

    d.   What did the Israelites know had occurred when the high priest came out of the tabernacle? (See vv. 17 – 19.)

    e.   Symbolically, what did the scapegoat carry away? (See vv. 20 – 22, 34.)

2.   What parallel exists between the animals sacrificed on the Day of Atonement and the sacrifice of Jesus' life for the sins of all humankind? (See Leviticus 16:20 – 22, 27 – 28; Matthew 27:31 – 33; John 19:17; Hebrews 13:11 – 13.)

3.   When the high priest returned from the most holy place in the tabernacle on the Day of Atonement, the Israelites knew that God had accepted their sacrifice (Leviticus 16:17). What

happened after Jesus' death on the cross that demonstrated God's acceptance of Jesus' sacrifice as the sinless Lamb of God? (See Matthew 28:1 – 10; Mark 16:1 – 7.)

4. What did the sacrifice of Jesus, the sinless Lamb of God, accomplish that the atonement sacrifices offered by the priests could not? (See John 1:29; 3:16; Hebrews 9:22 – 28; 10:11 – 14; 1 John 1:7; 3:5.)

Reflection

God, who brings *shalom* (order, purpose, harmony) into the chaos of our sinful world, established the tabernacle rituals in order to fuel the commitment and passion of the Israelites' relationship with him. He longed to live among his people and share a close relationship with them. As their God and "husband," he wanted to be a vital part of their everyday lives. He wanted their relationship with him to be the focus of their hearts and minds.

As you have become more familiar with the building of the tabernacle and its function in the lives of the Israelites, what have you discovered that is particularly meaningful to you:

In relationship to God's faithfulness in loving and redeeming his people?

Regarding the intimacy of the Israelites' relationship with God?

About God's ultimate plan to send the Messiah to atone for the sins of all humanity?

In what way has the tabernacle ritual, specifically the Day of Atonement, helped you to more fully know (experience) what Jesus accomplished on your behalf through his sacrificial death and resurrection?

In what ways will this more intimate experience impact your relationship with God? Your daily life?

Day Four | God "Re-Creates" His World

The Very Words of God

Observe my Sabbaths and have reverence for my sanctuary. I am the LORD. If you follow my decrees and are careful to obey my commands … I will look on you with favor and make you fruitful and increase your numbers, and I will keep my covenant with you…. I will put my dwelling place among you, and I will not abhor you. I will walk among you and be your God, and you will be my people. I am the LORD your God, who brought you out of Egypt so that you would no longer be slaves to the Egyptians; I broke the bars of your yoke and enabled you to walk with heads held high.

Leviticus 26:2–3, 9, 11–13

Bible Discovery

The Tabernacle: A "Re-Creation" to Restore His Shalom

"In the beginning, God created ... and it was very good" (Genesis 1:1, 31). But ever since that moment, the chaos of sin has been at work to destroy God's perfect creation. As wickedness multiplied throughout the earth, God implemented a plan to work in and through his people to "re-create" his creation — to restore the *shalom* (order, purpose, and harmony) that he created.

God, for example, used the great flood to "cleanse" his creation from evil and chose Noah as his partner in "re-creating" a world that was not in bondage to evil. And when he delivered the Hebrews from bondage in Egypt, God desired to "re-create" a people who would live in intimate relationship with him and participate in his plan to restore *shalom*. But living in a kingdom ruled by chaos for four hundred years had left its mark on God's people. They needed help to learn how to become the kingdom of priests God wanted them to be. So God provided the Torah and the tabernacle to teach them how to live in intimate relationship with him and display his character to the world.

1. After speaking to the chaos and bringing about order, how pleased was God with his original creation? (See Genesis 1:25 – 27, 31.)

2. Why did God send the great flood to destroy the earth during the time of Noah? (See Genesis 6:5 – 7.)

3. After the flood, God made promises and gave commands to
    the people who survived, almost as if he was starting over
    and "re-creating" a world where his *shalom* would reign.

    a. Using the following chart, compare God's instructions
        and blessings in Genesis 1:26 – 30 to those in Genesis
        9:1 – 3, 7 – 11:

Creation: Gen. 1:26 – 30	The "New" Creation after the Flood: Gen. 9:1 – 3, 7 – 11

    b. God gave the Torah to the Israelites, in part, to provide
        them with the background and knowledge they would
        need to become his "partners" in restoring *shalom* to his
        world. In light of the creation and flood accounts above,
        what sense of God's purpose do you think the Israel-
        ites would have recognized from God's instructions in
        Exodus 25:8; 29:42 – 46 and Leviticus 26:2 – 5, 9 – 13?

FOR GREATER UNDERSTANDING

As Westerners, we tend to view biblical stories as separate and unrelated. But the Eastern mind sees connections and gains insight from parallel events. So consider the message of "re-creation" and restoration of *shalom* that can be seen through the ark and great flood and the context in which the tabernacle was built and used.

Events Leading Up to, and Including, the Ark and Great Flood	Events Leading Up to, and Including, the Building of the Tabernacle
Set in water, a biblical metaphor for chaos (Gen. 1:2; 7:11)	Set in desert, a biblical metaphor for chaos (Deut. 8:15; 32:10)
Occurred in context of human wickedness—rebellion against God (Gen. 6:5–7)	Occurred in context of the Hebrews worshiping Egyptian gods (Ezek. 20:6–12; Ex. 32–33)
Unrighteous people not heeding God's call destroyed by water (chaos); righteous who obeyed God delivered through water (Gen. 7:23)	Egyptian army destroyed by Red Sea; righteous Hebrews miraculously saved through water (Ex. 14:26–30)
Righteous leader, Noah, favored by God and chosen to participate in God's plan to restore his world (Gen. 6:8–22)	Righteous leader, Moses, favored by God and chosen to participate in God's plan to restore his world (Ex. 33:12–17)
God designed ark, obedient people built it, and people were enabled to face the chaos of water he was leading them into (Gen. 6:14, 22)	God designed tabernacle, obedient people built it, and people were enabled to face the chaos of desert he was leading them into (Ex. 39:32, 42–43)
Ark was opened on first day of new calendar year (Gen. 8:13)	Tabernacle was set up on the first day of Hebrews' new calendar year (Ex. 40:2)
Noah and his family made sacrifice to God, who saved them (Gen. 8:20–22)	Hebrews made sacrifice to God, who saved them (Ex. 24:4–7)
God made a covenant with those he saved (Gen. 9:8–17)	God made a covenant with those he saved (Ex. 24:3–8)
God establishes community of Noah's descendants, 70 nations, to be his witnesses to his world (Gen. 10; 46:27)	God establishes community of 70 Hebrews, Abraham's descendants, to be his witnesses to the world (Gen. 46:27; Ex. 1:5)

4. Jewish thought has recognized a connection between the
    construction of the tabernacle (sanctuary) and the creation
    of the universe (Psalm 78:69). In what ways might the idea
    that God is, in a sense, "re-creating" his world through the
    tabernacle metaphor be supported by:

    a. The day of the year that the tabernacle was erected for
        the first time? (See Exodus 40:17.)

    b. The day of the year that Noah "uncovered" the ark and the
        human race began making a fresh start? (See Genesis 8:13.)

5. God spoke the universe into being in six days (Genesis 1:3–5,
    6–8, 9–13, 14–19, 20–23, 24–31) and proclaimed the seventh
    day to be the Sabbath, his day of rest (Genesis 2:2–3). What
    similar pattern do you notice in God's instructions to Moses
    regarding the building, or "creation," of the tabernacle? (See
    Exodus 25:1; 30:11, 17, 22, 34; 31:1, 12.)

    What do you think this connection communicated to the
    Israelites about how God was fulfilling his purpose through
    them?

    What do you think God was communicating to the Israelites
    concerning the importance of keeping the Sabbath? (See
    Exodus 20:8 – 11; 31:12 – 17; Leviticus 26:2.)

POINT TO PONDER

God clearly wanted the Israelites to view his instructions for building the tabernacle as a parallel to his work of creation. In fact, the creation story (first recorded in the Torah) was written specifically to them. Imagine their awe as they realized that the very God who created all things had delivered them from Egypt and was leading them through the desert! Not only that, their God wanted to live among them and wanted them to be his "partners" in restoring *shalom* to his world. As you read the following passages, just imagine what it must have been like for the Israelites to realize the significance of the tabernacle and what God was accomplishing through it and through them.

God's Creation of the Universe	The "Creation" (Construction) of the Tabernacle
Gen. 1:31: "God ... had made"	Ex. 25:8: "Then have them make"
Gen. 1:31: "God saw all"	Ex. 39:43: "Moses ... saw"
Gen. 2:1: "heavens and the earth were completed"	Ex. 39:32: "so all the work on the tabernacle ... was completed"
Gen. 2:2: "God had finished"	Ex. 40:33: "Moses finished the work"
Gen. 2:3: "And God blessed"	Ex. 39:43: "So Moses blessed"
Gen. 2:3: "and made it holy"	Ex. 40:9: "and it will be holy"

Reflection

Like the people of the Bible, we must learn that the only means to defeat the chaos of sin in our world are the means God provides for us in Jesus, the sacred biblical text, the power of his Spirit, and the encouragement of his community. These, like the ark and great flood for Noah and the tabernacle for the Israelites, bring us into an intimate relationship with God that enables us to become his partners in his plan to restore *shalom* to his world.

As you learned about God's plan to "re-create" his world through the events of the flood and the building and use of the tabernacle, what picture did you gain of what God is doing today to restore *shalom* to the chaos of your world?

How do you think he is changing the hearts and lives of his people (including your heart and life) to:

Restore their (your) relationship with him?

Empower them (you) to stand against chaos in the world?

Better display his character to a watching world?

Through the events of Mount Sinai and the lessons of the tabernacle, God taught the Israelites how to live in relationship with him. Over time, they became responsive and obedient to his words and overjoyed at his presence among them.

How committed are you to allowing God to "re-create" you to become part of his kingdom of priests in a spiritually needy world?

Which areas of chaos in your life create distance in your relationship with God and make the transformation he desires to take place in your heart and life more difficult?

Which of God's commands must you be particularly careful to obey in order to experience an intimate relationship with him?

Memorize

Observe my Sabbaths and have reverence for my sanctuary. I am the
*L*ORD*. If you follow my decrees and are careful to obey my commands*
… I will put my dwelling place among you, and I will not abhor you.
I will walk among you and be your God, and you will be my people. I
*am the L*ORD *your God, who brought you out of Egypt so that you would*
no longer be slaves to the Egyptians; I broke the bars of your yoke and
enabled you to walk with heads held high.

Leviticus 26:2 – 3, 11 – 13

Day Five | Being God's Presence Today

The Very Words of God

*Love the L*ORD *your God with all your heart and with all your soul and*
with all your strength. These commandments that I give you today are
to be upon your hearts. Impress them on your children. Talk about
them when you sit at home and when you walk along the road, when
you lie down and when you get up. Tie them as symbols on your hands
and bind them on your foreheads. Write them on the doorframes of
your houses and on your gates.

Deuteronomy 6:5 – 9

Bible Discovery

Commissioned to Create Space for God

God has long desired for the people he created to become his partners in restoring *shalom* to all things. The ancient Hebrews were
part of that plan, but they needed to be trained and shaped into
a people who would love (obey) the Lord their God with all their
heart, soul, and strength and thereby fulfill his purpose. The tabernacle was part of that shaping process. As God lived among his
people, and as they worshiped him through the tabernacle rituals,
the tabernacle became God's lesson in how to create space for him
in every part of their lives. Today, followers of Jesus no longer worship God at a tabernacle where there is a dedicated space for God.
However, it is no less important for us to make space for him in our

lives if we are to be "a chosen people, a royal priesthood, a holy nation, a people belonging to God, that you may declare the praises of him who called you out of darkness into his wonderful light" (1 Peter 2:9).

1. God gave Moses instructions for building the tabernacle and creating a space where the God of Israel could live among his people. What could prevent God from filling this space? (See Exodus 32:7 - 10.)

2. After God punished the Israelites because they sinned against God by creating and worshiping the golden calf (Exodus 32:35), what did he say he would do because he was displeased with them? (See Exodus 33:1 - 6.)

    What did God promise Moses that he would do for his people? (See Exodus 33:12 - 17.)

    After the Israelites completed the space in the tabernacle for him to live, what did God do? (See Exodus 40:34 - 35; Leviticus 9:23 - 24.)

    What do these examples reveal to you about God's commitment to his promises and his willingness to forgive his people?

3. Where did God say he would live when his people built a sanctuary for him? (See Exodus 25:8.)

   Why is it significant that God promised to live *among* (and *within*) his people, not just live *in* the tabernacle?

   Where (hint: *who*) is God's tabernacle, his temple today? (See 1 Corinthians 6:19; Ephesians 2:19 – 22.)

   In what ways has your understanding of what it means for a follower of Jesus to be God's temple grown because of what you have learned about the tabernacle?

4. What parallels do you see between what God commanded the Israelites to be in their world and what he commands those who follow Jesus to be today?

The Role of the Israelites in Their World	The Role of Those Who Follow Jesus Today
Ex. 19:3–7:	Rom. 12:1–2:
	1 Cor. 1:2:
	Eph. 1:4:
	1 Peter 2:9–10:

5. Holiness is an essential component of "making space" for
    God in our lives. When we sin we are, in effect, not provid-
    ing the "space" in which to have an intimate relationship
    with our holy God. The Israelites brought sacrifices to the
    tabernacle to atone for their sin and to reestablish intimacy
    with God. What must God's people today do in order to
    maintain an intimate relationship with him? (See 1 John 1:9.)

Reflection

The Israelites obeyed all of God's commands and completed the tabernacle according to his specifications. In response, God filled the
space his people created, and the "holy nation" of his people went
on to show (imperfectly, however) the world what it was like to be
the treasured possession of God Almighty. In a similar way, those
of us who are followers of Jesus today can choose daily to create
"space" in our lives for God so that other people will see his love in
us and personally experience the transforming power of his awesome presence in their lives.

Read Galatians 5:22 – 25, which highlights the evidences of
God's Spirit that other people will experience in and through us
when we live in close relationship with our holy God.

In what ways is the fruit of the Spirit a display of what it
means to be a "priest" or "holy nation" to the world?

What do you think is the connection between "making
space" for God and "keep[ing] in step with the Spirit"?

In what way(s) do God's detailed tabernacle instructions help you to understand the work that is required to "make space" for God in your life?

What might have happened if God's people had refused to donate materials for the construction of the tabernacle, had not helped to build it, or had built it differently than God commanded?

In what ways does your answer point out areas where you need to be more diligent in "making space" for God in your life?

What is your personal commitment to being the "tabernacle" or dwelling place of God's presence today?

Which specific things are essential for you to do in order to "make space" for God at all times — including your work, recreation, time with family and friends, etc.? (List them!)

Part of the benefit of the tabernacle ritual was that the essential practices of "making space" for God became a regular part of life. Review your list (page 97) and write down specific activities, times, and places that you will commit to "making space" for God in your life.

Memorize

For we are the temple of the living God. As God has said: "I will live with them and walk among them, and I will be their God, and they will be my people." ... Since we have these promises, dear friends, let us purify ourselves from everything that contaminates body and spirit, perfecting holiness out of reverence for God.

2 Corinthians 6:16; 7:1

HE LED THEM LIKE A SHEPHERD

The Hebrews found themselves living in Egypt after Jacob and his family went there to escape a famine that gripped the entire Middle East. In Egypt the family was reconciled to Joseph, the long-lost brother who had become Pharaoh's deputy. Through Joseph's influence, the family settled in Goshen, some of Egypt's finest agricultural land. Although no records describe the lives of these descendants of Abraham during most of the four centuries they spent in Egypt, we know that God blessed them and that they became numerous and prosperous. But they also became Egyptian in many ways. They even drifted away from the God of their fathers and worshiped Egyptian gods (Ezekiel 20:6 – 8).

God did not forget them, however. Ever since Adam and Eve sinned, he has been working out his plan to break the power of sin and the chaos it brings into his world. He is working to restore *shalom* (order, peace, and harmony) to his creation. Amazingly this plan involves using human beings — the very creatures who originally set loose the chaos — and the Hebrews were part of that plan. When the Egyptians became afraid of the Hebrews and enslaved them, causing them to suffer greatly, it was time for God to unfold the next step in restoring *shalom* to his broken world. God heard the Hebrews' cries and with demonstrations of great power delivered them from the chaos of Egypt. He then led them into the desert where he began to shape them into becoming his witnesses to the world.

God's desire is for his people to become his witnesses who display his character by their every thought, word, and action. Therefore, the leadership style of those God chooses to lead his people is very important. But the leadership the Hebrews had experienced in Egypt could be harsh and cruel. It benefited the powerful at the expense of the weak. In contrast, God's leadership exemplifies the caring, gentle leadership of a shepherd.

So in order to show the world how God leads, the Hebrews had to learn to lead as he leads. It wouldn't be easy. They not only had to leave Egypt physically, but they had to replace the worldview and values of Egypt that were embedded in their hearts with those of God. Perhaps this is why Jewish tradition has always emphasized that it took much less "effort" on God's part to get his chosen people out of Egypt than it did to get Egypt out of them!

While God shaped his people, he also shaped their leaders. He chose from among the people leaders who walked obediently with him and shared his heart for the "sheep." Slowly, patiently, God molded these leaders to demonstrate his character (not without occasional failure) to the rest of the Hebrew people. He instilled in them the faith they would need to trust and obey him fully. He taught them to follow his example and lead the people as a shepherd would lead them. By their obedience, these leaders — Moses, Aaron, Joshua, Phineas, and many whose names we do not even know — contributed to history's understanding of God and his style of leadership.

Even as God patiently molded Moses and other leaders, it was apparent that another leader, a sinless one, was needed to display God fully, in all his glory. The successes and failures of the ancient leaders would point us toward that leader. He would be another Moses, another high priest like Aaron, another Joshua (even bearing that name) — like these men but greater, leading like the Chief Shepherd he was. So as we walk with God's people in the desert, let's focus on how God "led them like sheep through the desert" (Psalm 78:52). Let's allow ourselves to be reminded of the greater leader — the Messiah — the sinless Shepherd who encourages us to lead as he leads.

Opening Thoughts (3 minutes)

The Very Words of God

> *We will tell the next generation the praiseworthy deeds of the LORD, his power, and the wonders he has done....*
>
> *He brought his people out like a flock; he led them like sheep through the desert.*

Psalm 78:4, 52

Think About It

People today give speeches, conduct seminars, and write articles and books about leadership. They often focus on what leadership is, the pros and cons of various leadership styles, or how to train oneself to be a better leader.

If God were giving a seminar on leadership, what do you think would be his focus, and in what ways might his message differ from that of human "experts"?

DVD Notes (29 minutes)

Two sticks, two kinds of leadership

God chooses Moses to lead as God leads

God's purpose is to end the suffering of chaos and restore *shalom*

Moses needs training in God's way of leadership

Why choose the desert for training?

DVD Discussion (7 minutes)

1. Using the map on page 103, locate Goshen and Canaan. Approximately how many miles is Canaan from Egypt?

   Next locate the traditional Israelite route, Jebel Musa (the traditional Mount Sinai), Desert of Sin, Desert of Paran, Timnah, Kadesh Barnea, and Desert of Zin. Approximately how large is the area in which the Israelites wandered for forty years?

How does this change your perception of the Israelites' training by God in the desert?

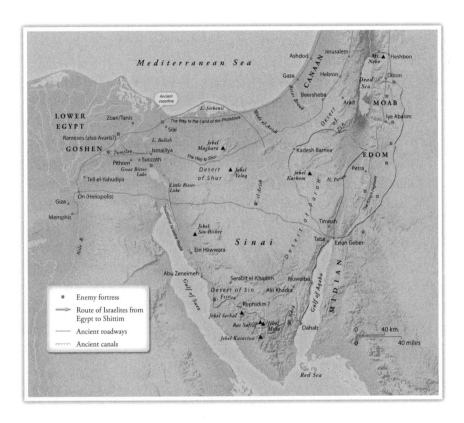

2. When you consider all of the ability and leadership training
    that Moses had acquired, why do you think he viewed him-
    self as so unqualified for the task God assigned to him?

Which experiences and abilities might Moses have thought
made him less qualified to lead the Hebrews out of Egypt?

In what ways might these perceived weaknesses actually have made him more qualified?

3. Moses was well acquainted with the power of Pharaoh's "stick." What do you think went through his mind when God entrusted him with a "stick" that represented God's divine authority and power?

4. Which words did God use to describe his kind of leadership, and in what ways does it differ from the kind of leadership that was exhibited at Timnah? From the kind of leadership common in your culture?

5. In what ways has this brief exposure to the desert, the land of the shepherd, helped you to understand why God chose it to be a training ground for his people and their leaders?

What do you think people can learn in the desert better than anywhere else?

THESE TWO PHOTOS EXEMPLIFY THE CONTRAST BETWEEN LEADERSHIP IN THE KINGDOM OF CHAOS AS DEMONSTRATED BY PHARAOH, AND LEADERSHIP IN GOD'S KINGDOM AS PORTRAYED BY A SHEPHERD LEADING THE SHEEP.

PROFILE OF A CULTURE
Understanding the Power of Pharaoh

The title *Pharaoh*, given to ancient Egyptian kings, actually means "great house." The word apparently referred to the palace and over time came to mean "king."

As the theological leader of Egyptian culture, Pharaoh was believed to be a divine element of the universe and a living descendant of the sun god Re. Pharaoh, sanctioned by Egypt's other gods, was believed to be responsible for maintaining the divine order of the universe — including the Nile River and its annual flood. Without his contribution, it was believed that the world would descend into chaos.

Anyone who opposed Pharaoh did so at great peril. Pharaoh wielded absolute power and authority over Egypt and its people — and many foreigners. Hundreds, perhaps thousands, of ancient carvings depict Pharaoh holding a flail, crook, or other "stick" (identifying him as lord and god), and beating his enemies or bashing in the skulls of helpless prisoners whom he holds by their hair. Other carvings show piles of human hands, phalli, and tongues being presented to Pharaoh to glorify his divine power over all opposition. When the Hebrews were enslaved in Egypt, they experienced the crushing blows of the brute force of Pharaoh's kingdom. They were worked ruthlessly and were forced to throw their newborn boys into the Nile.

Small Group Bible Discovery and Discussion (15 minutes)

Leadership in God's Kingdom vs. Leadership in the Kingdom of Chaos

Behind the story of the exodus is the story of two kingdoms in conflict. First, there is the kingdom of God. Its purpose is to restore *shalom* — order, purpose, harmony — into the chaos of a broken world. Then there is the anti-kingdom, the kingdom of the Evil One that brought the chaos of sin into God's creation. In this story, the anti-kingdom is represented by Egypt and its gods as personified in Pharaoh. Each kingdom promises to bring order out of chaos, *shalom* out of evil. One will eventually fulfill what it promises; the other will actually add to the chaos. Let's take a look at the contrasting leadership values of each kingdom.

1. Genesis 1 and 2 summarize the story of God establishing order (*shalom*) out of chaos by creating the universe and populating the earth with living things. In Genesis 3, the influence of the Evil One quickly turned this beautiful order back into chaos.

    a. What was God's plan to destroy evil and restore *shalom* to his creation, and who had God chosen to help accomplish this plan? (See Genesis 12:1 – 3.)

    b. What connection would exist between the people God chose to help fulfill his plan and the kingdom of chaos? (See Genesis 15:13 – 18; 46:2 – 4.)

    c. What kind of influence would the kingdom of chaos have on God's people, and what would God do about it? (See Exodus 1:5 – 11; Joshua 24:14; Ezekiel 20:4 – 11.)

2. When faced with adversity, or when threatened, what differences do you see between the objectives and type of leadership exhibited by Moses (representing God and his kingdom) and those of Pharaoh (representing the kingdom of chaos)? (See Exodus 1:8 – 22; 5:22 – 6:8.)

In what ways do these two examples of leadership in action help you to better understand the kind of leadership God values?

Which contrasting examples of leadership in your world help to remind you of the differences between leadership in God's kingdom and leadership in the kingdom of chaos?

PROFILE OF A CULTURE
Crook and Flail: Symbols of Pharaoh's Authority

As symbols of Pharaoh's authority to rule his kingdom, the flail and shepherd's crook represented Pharaoh's power, royalty, and deity. In carvings and statues, the flail and crook were usually held, one in each hand, across the chest of Pharaoh or the god Osiris.

Flail. A flail was an agricultural tool used to thresh grain. It was made from two or more sticks attached to each other with a chain or rope. After spreading grain on the ground, a farmer would hold one stick of the flail and swing the other(s) repeatedly to hit the grain and separate it from the husk. The flail had other uses as well. Soldiers used flails as effective weapons, and the Egyptians used them to hurt enemy captives and slaves.

Because flails were a sign of power, Pharaoh is frequently depicted holding a flail as a symbol of his office. The flail also illustrated his role as the personification of Osiris, the god who was believed to cause the Nile to flood and crops to grow. A flail pictured in Pharaoh's hand typically had three attached sticks.

Crook. In hieroglyphics, the crook symbol represented rule. Scholars believe the use of the shepherd's crook as a symbol of deity, power, and authority dates back to the herding culture of very ancient Egypt. As a shepherd ruled the flock or herd and was obligated to provide for it, so Pharaoh had abso-

THESE COLOSSI (STATUES) STAND ON BOTH SIDES OF THE ENTRANCE TO THE HYPOSTYLE HALL IN THE RAMESSEUM, THE FUNERARY TEMPLE OF RAMSES THE GREAT. THE NOW HEADLESS STATUES SHOW PHARAOH'S CROSSED HANDS HOLDING THE SHEPHERD'S CROOK AND FLAIL TO SYMBOLIZE HIS ROYALTY, ABSOLUTE AUTHORITY, AND DIVINE POWER.

lute authority and responsibility to maintain order — *ma'at* — for the benefit of his people. Eventually reduced to the size of a scepter, the crook often appeared in statuary of the monarchy and many of the gods, particularly Osiris.

3. After allowing his people to become slaves in Egypt and experience the suffering inflicted by the kingdom of chaos, what did God do to begin to teach them about his kingdom and shape them into participants and leaders in his plan of restoration? (See Deuteronomy 8:1 – 5; Ezekiel 20:5 – 12.)

How different was this new environment for them?

Why do you think they kept wanting to go back to Egypt?

DID YOU KNOW?
Moses' Staff: Representing the Authority of God's Kingdom

In contrast to the brute force symbolized by Pharaoh's crook and flail, Moses and Aaron each carried a staff typically used by shepherds. In one sense, that staff constantly reminded Moses how he was to lead. In another sense, it represented God's authority and demonstrated his awesome power over all of creation.

The image of a shepherd leading the flock was very strong in the culture of God's people during biblical times, and God is often compared to a shepherd leading a flock. (See Genesis 48:15; Psalms 23:1–3; 78:52; 79:13; 80:1; 95:7; Isaiah 40:11.) Jewish sages taught that a shepherd leads primarily by word, so naturally the words "desert," "leader," "word," "speak," and "shepherd" come from the same Hebrew root word, *dbr*. Even today, shepherds in the Middle East normally do not drive their sheep ahead of them. Instead, they walk in front and lead their flocks by speaking to them. It is compelling to watch a shepherd, ahead of a large flock of sheep and goats, talking continually and leading the flock toward its destination.

The shepherd provided the image of how God wanted Moses to lead his people, and the staff was the evidence of the shepherd's authority to lead. That's why it was so important for Moses to know that God himself was the power and authority behind his "stick." When God told Moses to throw his staff on the ground and it became a snake (Exodus 4:3), Moses no doubt understood that only God's power could have transformed it—that certainly wasn't something Moses was capable of doing.

It is interesting to note that God sent Moses to Pharaoh to speak to him. It was only when Pharaoh refused to listen (Exodus 5:1 – 2) that Moses' staff became an instrument of the Lord's power in the confrontation between the kingdom of God and the kingdom of chaos, as represented by Pharaoh and Egypt's gods. Pharaoh certainly understood that the contest between Aaron's staff and the staffs of Pharaoh's magicians (Exodus 7:8 – 12) represented a serious confrontation of power and authority between himself and Egypt's gods on one hand, and the God of the Hebrews on the other.

Faith Lesson (5 minutes)

God gave his ancient people such leaders as Moses, Aaron, Joshua, and David who, although they were imperfect, still exemplified the kind of leadership God values. God has also given us Jesus, the sinless and supreme example of leadership that truly represents God's kingdom (Matthew 26:47 – 54, John 18:36 – 37, and Philippians 2:5 – 11 provide a few examples of Jesus' leadership in action). Today, God calls every person who follows (obeys) him to demonstrate the leadership displayed by a wise and compassionate desert shepherd as opposed to the ruthless and violent leadership of a Pharaoh. We may not have actually seen a desert shepherd calling to and leading a flock, but we can recognize some of the shepherd's characteristics: concern for each individual, not just the group; kindness; compassion; leading by example in front; guiding the flock to food and water; protecting the flock from danger; etc.

1. In what ways do Jesus' leadership methods, including his use of power, differ from those of earthly "kingdoms," including the leadership methods of your culture?

2. In what specific ways has your culture — as a representation of the kingdom of chaos — shaped your personal leadership values and methods?

    As you reflect on your leadership values and how you express them in your dealings with your family, neighbors, coworkers, and friends, which kingdom would they say you serve?

    Why is it so easy to try to bring about God's ways by using our own leadership techniques rather than obeying and trusting in him and the power of his Word?

    What makes it possible to live in and influence your culture without losing sight of your calling to display God in such a way that all the world may come to know him?

3. How deep is your commitment to serve God and his kingdom as a shepherd serves, to being his witness who displays his character and brings his *shalom* into a world of chaos?

PROFILE OF TWO CULTURES
Leadership in Conflict

Kingdom of Egypt	Kingdom of God
Based on false gods and the power of evil as personified in Pharaoh, the ruler of Egypt	Based on the all-powerful Creator God — who is holy, loving, compassionate, and without sin
Promised to make order out of chaos but actually increased the chaos for those who were not in power	Brings *shalom* (order, harmony, purpose) into the chaos of our broken world and ultimately will restore all of God's creation
Extended its influence by threats and suffering; enslaved some and even threw babies into the Nile River	Provides protection for the weak, widowed, poor, and orphaned, and extends its influence by being willing to suffer on behalf of others
Leadership was symbolized by the Pharaoh's staff that hit and crushed people	Leadership is symbolized by the shepherd's staff that gently led — and still leads — God's "flock" to safety

Closing (1 minute)

Read aloud together Psalm 78:4, 13 – 16, 52: "We will tell the next generation the praiseworthy deeds of the LORD, his power, and the wonders he has done. . . . He divided the sea and led them through; he made the water stand firm like a wall. He guided them with the cloud by day and with light from the fire all night. He split the rocks in the desert and gave them water as abundant as the seas; he brought streams out of a rocky crag and made water flow down like rivers. . . . He brought his people out like a flock; he led them like sheep through the desert."

Then pray that God will help you to focus your thoughts and actions on him — on what he has done for his people and how he leads them. Ask him to help you be the kind of leader God desires you to be — in your home, neighborhood, at work, in your community, and with friends. Ask him to empower you to be courageous in standing for his kingdom rather than the chaos of evil in our world.

Memorize

We will tell the next generation the praiseworthy deeds of the LORD, his power, and the wonders he has done....

He divided the sea and led them through; he made the water stand firm like a wall.

He guided them with the cloud by day and with light from the fire all night.

He split the rocks in the desert and gave them water as abundant as the seas; he brought streams out of a rocky crag and made water flow down like rivers....

He brought his people out like a flock; he led them like sheep through the desert.

Psalm 78:4, 13 – 16, 52

Learning to Live by the Word and Heart of God

In-Depth Personal Study Sessions

Day One | God Leads Like a Shepherd

The Very Words of God

> *He tends his flock like a shepherd: He gathers the lambs in his arms and carries them close to his heart; he gently leads those that have young.*
>
> **Isaiah 40:11**

Bible Discovery

God Reveals Himself as the Shepherd of His People

Through the Spirit-empowered leadership of Moses, God led his chosen people out of the lush, fertile farms of Egypt and into the vast desert wilderness. Even today, the Sinai Desert is a maze of steep rocky mountains, trackless canyons, and sand-choked valleys. Although the Bedouin nomads navigate the region with ease (as Moses would have after tending sheep there for forty years), it is a threatening world to those who are unfamiliar with it as the Hebrews were. No wonder they were afraid they would die in the desert. They were totally dependent on both God's provision of manna,

IMAGINE HOW IMPORTANT IT WAS FOR THE HEBREWS TO HAVE A WISE, CARING SHEPHERD TO LEAD THEM THROUGH THE VAST, WILDERNESS DESERTS OF THE SINAI. WHAT OPPORTUNITIES WOULD GOD HAVE IN DESERTS LIKE THIS TO SHOW HIS PEOPLE THE KIND OF LEADERSHIP HE VALUES?

quail, and water, and his faithfulness in leading them through the dangerous and unknown land.

1. The image of a shepherd is familiar to people living in the lands of the Middle East. As you read the following Scripture portions, notice how this image is used to describe God's relationship with his people, especially the manner in which he led them during their years in the desert. Take careful note of the things God does, provides, and desires for his flock and what those details reveal about the kind of leader God is.

Text	What God Does/Provides/ Desires	God as a Shepherd Leader
Ps. 23:1–4		
Ps. 77:19–20		
Ps. 78:52–55		
Ps. 100:3		
Isa. 40:10–11		
Jer. 31:10		

2. After the Hebrews marched out of Egypt, God anticipated and met their need for his guiding, protective presence — in much the same way a shepherd would guide a flock. In each of the following passages what specific examples of shepherd-like care did God provide for his people?

Exodus 13:17 - 18, 21 - 22

Exodus 14:19 - 20

Exodus 15:23 - 27

Numbers 9:15 - 23

Deuteronomy 1:30 - 33

Why do you think it was important for the Israelites to actually see and experience God's leading?

In what ways do you think these examples helped them to know their God and trust him as their shepherd?

THINK ABOUT IT

English Bibles say that the pillar of fire and cloud "went ahead of" the Hebrews (Exodus 13:21–22), but the Hebrew verb used, *halak*, literally means "walked." So to the Hebrews, it was as if the pillar of cloud "walked" ahead of them — on legs!

The Bible describes the cloud of God's glory as "staying" or "standing" at the entrance to the tabernacle (as in Exodus 33:9–10 and Numbers 12:5). In these instances, the Hebrew word translated "stay" literally means "stand." The image of the pillar of cloud "standing" before the tabernacle as if on legs communicates God's presence in a powerful way.

God's presence with the Israelites in the desert was not merely an abstract idea. Day in and day out they could see the visual reminder that God was with them. They could see that he was guiding and protecting them like a shepherd.

This image was so significant in the minds of the Israelites that when Solomon built God's temple in Jerusalem, he placed two columns in front of the entrance (2 Chronicles 3:15–17). Jewish tradition views these columns as representing God's legs.

GOLDEN PILLARS BY THE ENTRANCE TO SOLOMON'S TEMPLE REMINDED THE ISRAELITES OF THE PILLAR OF FIRE AND CLOUD THAT "WALKED" AHEAD OF THEM IN THE DESERT.

3. Scripture portrays God as "dwelling" in the clouds, and on numerous occasions he descended to his people in a cloud. This image helped to communicate to the Israelites that God, who dwells in heaven, had come down to live among his people where he could lead them as a shepherd would lead a flock.

   a. What would happen when the cloud of God's presence descended? (See Exodus 16:10 – 12; 19:9, 16 – 20; 33:7 – 11; 34:4 – 8.)

   b. What special communication would God deliver from the cloud of his presence in the holy of holies, and how seriously were the Israelites to view his presence there? (See Exodus 25:22; Leviticus 16:2.)

   c. In keeping with the shepherd-and-flock image, what do you think God, the shepherd, was trying to teach the Israelites, his flock, during their years in the desert? (See Deuteronomy 8:2 – 4.)

4. Which metaphor for leadership did God use to describe people who led his people on his behalf? (See 2 Samuel 5:1 – 2; Jeremiah 23:2 – 4; 50:6; Ezekiel 34:1 – 2, 7 – 10.)

   What do these passages say to you about God's faithfulness as a shepherd in providing for his people?

How seriously does God view the responsibility of those who represent him in caring for his people?

Reflection

Many generations after the exodus, Nehemiah was supervising the rebuilding of Jerusalem following the Babylonian captivity. At that time, the people offered praise to God for all that he had done throughout Israel's history. Their recounting of God's loving, faithful care of his people during the exodus is a beautiful picture of what it means to be a shepherd of God's flock. Take time to read and meditate on Nehemiah 9:9 – 21. As you read this passage, write down all of the qualities of a good shepherd that you see demonstrated by God's care for his people during the exodus. Then write down how God has been your shepherd and demonstrated these qualities in your life, particularly during your difficult "desert experiences."

The Qualities of a Good Shepherd	How God Has Been My Shepherd

In what way(s) do you think the desert experiences of the Israelites made them more aware of God as their shepherd?

In what ways did those experiences give them opportunities to learn how to follow him?

How aware are you of your need for God's "shepherding" as you navigate through life?

What changes must you make in order to be less "stiff-necked" than the Israelites were as God seeks to lead you and teach you to listen for his voice and follow his commands?

Memorize

Because of your great compassion you did not abandon them in the desert. By day the pillar of cloud did not cease to guide them on their path, nor the pillar of fire by night to shine on the way they were to take. You gave your good Spirit to instruct them. You did not withhold your manna from their mouths, and you gave them water for their thirst. For forty years you sustained them in the desert.

Nehemiah 9:19–21

Day Two | God Chooses Moses

The Very Words of God

> *But Moses said to God, "Who am I, that I should go to Pharaoh and*
> *bring the Israelites out of Egypt?"*
> *And God said, "I will be with you. And this will be the sign to you that it*
> *is I who have sent you: When you have brought the people out of Egypt,*
> *you will worship God on this mountain."*
>
> *Exodus 3:11–12*

Bible Discovery

What "Qualified" Moses for Leadership?

When we think about what qualifies a person for leadership, we
might list such things as an advanced university degree, the ability
to speak well, a network of influential people, experience in dealing
with the media, years of training, and the like. Moses had qualifications such as these. When he met God at the burning bush, Moses
had lived in the palace in Egypt as Pharaoh's adopted son, knew
Egyptian life and culture, spoke the language, probably knew many
high-ranking officials, understood Egypt's religious beliefs, knew
its geography, and apparently knew his Hebrew roots. In addition,
Moses had spent forty years being a shepherd in the very desert
through which God wanted him to lead Israel to their new land
(Acts 7:23–32). Moses knew all of the routes and the people who
lived there; he knew where to find the best grazing areas, springs,
and wells.

From a human perspective, no one could have been more qualified
to fulfill the task God had in mind! God had groomed Moses pre-
cisely for this mission. Even Moses' name in Hebrew, *moshe*, means
"to draw out" — a prediction of how God would use him to lead
the Hebrews out of slavery and the Egyptian worldview they had
adopted. But is this why God chose him?

1. Because she was chosen to be his nurse, we know that
   Moses spent his earliest years with his Hebrew mother
   before he began living in the royal household of Egypt
   as Pharaoh's adopted son. During his adult years, which

people — the Hebrews or the Egyptians — did Moses identify
with as his own? (See Exodus 2:10; Hebrews 11:24 – 25.)

Why do you think he made that choice?

What does this choice reveal about Moses' character and the
values closest to his heart?

2. Acts 7:20 – 28 and Exodus 3:7 – 12 provide two very different
   perceptions of Moses' qualifications and his confidence in
   their value to the task of rescuing the Hebrews from Egypt.

   a. What qualifications for success do we know Moses pos-
      sessed? (See Acts 7:20 – 22.)

   b. What confidence did Moses have in his earthly qualifi-
      cations, and for what purpose did he seek to use them?
      (See Acts 7:23 – 25.)

   c. When Moses met God at Mount Horeb and God
      explained what he was asking Moses to do, what doubts

immediately surfaced in Moses' mind? (See Exodus 3:7 – 11.)

d. On the basis of which qualifications did God say Moses' success would depend? In what ways do you think this is, or is not, the answer Moses expected? In what ways is it what you expected? (See Exodus 3:12.)

THINK ABOUT IT

When God spoke to Moses from the burning bush on Mount Horeb and explained what giant task he was choosing him to accomplish, Moses was so overwhelmed that he claimed he couldn't speak (Exodus 3:11 – 4:13). No matter that a much younger Moses was known for being "powerful" in speech (Acts 7:22). Why was Moses so reluctant to tell people what God had to say?

Before we judge Moses harshly, perhaps we should consider the similar responses of two other prophets: Isaiah and Jeremiah. When they were commissioned to speak God's words to others, they too felt overwhelmed by their inadequacy (Isaiah 6:5 – 9; Jeremiah 1:4 – 9). To speak God's words to others is an awesome responsibility. We dare not do it unless we know God is with us!

3. The Bible tells us that while we tend to greatly value what we see on the outside of a person, God values what is in a person's heart (1 Samuel 16:7). Perhaps this perspective can help us recognize some of the qualifications for leadership that God may have seen in Moses. As you read the following passages, write down the values and character you see expressed by God and by Moses.

Characteristics of God	Characteristics of Moses
Ex. 2:24–25; 3:7–9; 4:31; Deut. 16:20; Ezek. 9:9–10	Ex. 2:11–13
Ex. 12:12–13, 29	Ex. 2:15–17
Ps. 23:1–2	Ex. 5:19–23
John 3:16; Rom. 5:4–9	Ex. 32:7–14
1 John 1:9	Ex. 32:30–35

What did you learn about the heart of Moses?

Why were Moses' passionate love for the Hebrews and his compassion for suffering people important qualifications in light of the leadership task God wanted him to accomplish?

Reflection

When God and Moses saw people suffering, they responded with tender hearts to meet the need. Jesus, too, responded with compassion to the cries of those who suffered (Mark 10:46–52). And in 1 John 2:5–6, those who follow Jesus are called to do the same. So consider the status of your heart and the role it plays in your leadership — in your home, with coworkers and/or neighbors, in your larger community, and even beyond your country.

In what ways are the following "qualifications" that Moses demonstrated evident in your heart and in your dealings with other people? What may God be doing in your life to help develop these qualities in you so that you have a more tender, godly heart:

- An intimate relationship with God

- Leading by speaking God's word to others

- Courageously and honestly "wrestling" with God when you are struggling to understand his ways

- Totally committed to leading God's people even when it requires personal sacrifice

- Being sensitive to the pain and needs of those who are weak or hurting

- Completely committed to living according to God's ways

- Modeling leadership as well as speaking it

- Raising up, training, and encouraging other people to lead God's people

Many of us cultivate our earthly leadership qualities far more than our "heart" qualities or our relationship with God. What risks do we face if we have more confidence in our earthly qualifications than we do in relying on God to help us do what he has called us to do?

When did this happen in Moses' life, and what resulted?

When has it happened in yours, and what resulted?

To what extent do you have a passionate desire to know God's heart more intimately?

What steps are you taking to develop a more loving, sensitive, and compassionate heart and to demonstrate that godly heart in everything you do, with everyone you meet?

Day Three | Lead as I Lead

The Very Words of God

Moses said to the LORD, "You have been telling me, 'Lead these people,' but you have not let me know whom you will send with me. You have said, 'I know you by name and you have found favor with me.' If you are pleased with me, teach me your ways so I may know you and continue to find favor with you. Remember that this nation is your people."

The LORD replied, "My Presence will go with you, and I will give you rest."

Exodus 33:12–14

Bible Discovery

Learning to Lead as God Leads

The exodus story is the story of two kingdoms, each with a distinct leadership style. One uses brute force to benefit those in power. Pharaoh used this style — crushing his enemies, working the Hebrew slaves brutally, condemning their infant boys to death in the Nile River. The leadership of the other kingdom is best portrayed by a loving shepherd who guides the flock by voice and cares tenderly for each of the sheep.

Moses grew up in Pharaoh's palace learning the first kind of leadership. He needed to learn the second style because that is how God typically leads, and it is what he desires from shepherds who lead on his behalf. So, with no idea what God had in store for his future, Moses spent forty years as a shepherd. During these years he became more and more like the shepherd leader God desired him to be. Imagine what Moses thought when God commissioned him — once a prince of Egypt and now a nomadic shepherd — to be like God in confronting the most powerful empire in the world and leading God's beloved Hebrews! How well had he learned to lead as the Good Shepherd leads?

1. Although Moses desired to identify with the Hebrew people of his birth and had compassion for them in their suffering, the fact is he grew up in Pharaoh's palace. What are the indications that the Egyptian worldview — including Pharaoh's brute-like style of leadership — may have become more a part of Moses than he realized? (See Exodus 2:11 – 19; Acts 7:23 – 29.)

2. When God first met Moses at the burning bush and commissioned him to speak to Pharaoh and lead the Hebrews out of Egypt, how did Moses respond? (See Exodus 3:1 – 11.)

Is this the same response you would have expected from Moses before he spent forty years tending sheep in the desert? What do you think changed?

Why do you think Moses responded this way?

3. What similarities do you see between the way a shepherd guides a flock — leading by walking ahead of them and calling to the sheep to show them the way — and the way God instructed Moses to confront Pharaoh and lead the Hebrews out of Egypt? (See Exodus 3:13 – 20; 4:1 – 9.)

What was the primary way Moses was to lead on God's behalf?

When was Moses to take action and demonstrate God's power?

How was Moses' staff (the symbol of a shepherd's verbal, caring leadership) to be used, and whose power did it represent?

PROFILE OF A LEADER
Moses Learns to Lead with the Power of a Shepherd

In contrast to Pharaoh's style of leadership, the godly and humble "shepherd" style of leadership that God taught Moses unleashes the greatest power of all — the power of the Creator of the universe. Although God can use his power to destroy any and all opposition, he often does not. Instead, as Moses and the Hebrews learned, God patiently leads by his words and gives people an opportunity to follow him.

Only when people continually ignore or reject his words will God use his power. Usually even that is done with a gentle mercy that invites people to repent, return to him, and receive his forgiveness. Over time Moses, the servant with a shepherd's heart like that of God, learned to lead as God leads. His leadership revealed to God's people — God's flock — the character of their eternal Shepherd. Using an imperfect man, God demonstrated to his flock his own perfect character. But Moses' human failings would eventually require a leader greater than Moses. That perfect, unblemished leader, "the Good Shepherd" (John 10:11 – 14), would come to show the nature of God's leadership to all humankind.

4. Even though Moses had a sensitive, compassionate heart that longed for justice, he did not learn overnight how to lead as God leads. That took time — not just time spent as a shepherd, but time spent observing God's example, time spent listening for God's voice, time spent getting to know God and his ways. Read the following passages and note the characteristics of Moses' relationship with God that would have helped him to know God and become a shepherd like him.

    Exodus 4:19 – 20

    Exodus 5:22 – 6:1; 17:4 – 6

Exodus 33:7 – 11, 13

Deuteronomy 34:10

Psalm 77:20

Reflection

Great leaders never forget that leadership is about being a godly person who leads as God leads. But in order to do this, we need to know God and experience a vital, intimate relationship with him. We need to not only devote ourselves to prayer and Bible study but to walk as he would walk in everyday life. We need to ask him to open our hearts (and our ears) to his guiding voice, and we need to follow his example by hearing and responding to the cries of God's flock.

These priorities for life and leadership in God's kingdom are summarized in the *shema*, what Jesus called the greatest commandment: "Hear, O Israel: The LORD our God, the LORD is one. Love the LORD your God with all your heart and with all your soul and with all your strength. These commandments that I give you today are to be upon your hearts" (Deuteronomy 6:4 – 6). As it is expressed in Hebrew, *hearing* means more than simply being aware of sounds. *Hearing* means to obey, to follow, to respond. The people whom God wants to shepherd his flock are people like Moses who passionately desire to hear as God hears.

How committed are you to developing an intensely personal relationship with God — one that requires all your heart, all your soul, and all your strength?

What are you doing to cultivate and maintain such a relationship?

How necessary is your obedience to God's commands in that relationship?

What cries of those who suffer or are oppressed do you hear?

How do you think God responds when he hears those same cries?

How do you think God wants you to respond, and are you willing to do it?

Moses was willing to offer himself as a sacrifice for the sins of God's "flock" — the Hebrews (Exodus 32:32). He of course couldn't because he himself was not without sin, but how much love must he have had for God's flock to offer this?

To what extent do you share the same kind of love that compelled Moses to be a shepherd leader?

What significant personal sacrifices are you willing to make for people who need help? For those who suffer?

Memorize

> *Hear, O Israel: The LORD our God, the LORD is one. Love the LORD your God with all your heart and with all your soul and with all your strength. These commandments that I give you today are to be upon your hearts.*

> *Deuteronomy 6:4–6*

Day Four | Trust: The Lesson of the Desert

The Very Words of God

> *It was because the LORD loved you and kept the oath he swore to your forefathers that he brought you out with a mighty hand and redeemed you from the land of slavery, from the power of Pharaoh king of Egypt. Know therefore that the LORD your God is God; he is the faithful God, keeping his covenant of love to a thousand generations of those who love him and keep his commands.*

> *Deuteronomy 7:8–9*

Bible Discovery

"Trust Me, Trust Me, Trust Me!"

It's easy for us to view the exodus as simply a change in locations — God moving his people from slavery in Egypt to freedom in the Promised Land with forty years of wandering in the middle. But that's not what God had in mind. When the Hebrews left Egypt, they could not survive, much less thrive, in the desert. They needed to learn to trust in the loving care of God their Shepherd and in the leaders he chose when they faced life-threatening dangers in the desert, such as intense heat and lack of good water and food. God used the desert to shape, train, and teach them to depend fully on him and live by every word he spoke. Only then could they become his priests and witnesses who would display him to other nations.

1. From the beginning of the exodus experience, even before the Hebrews left Egypt, they were learning what it meant to trust in their God. This was true for Moses and Aaron, as well as for the flock they led. As you read the following passages, notice how the stakes kept rising as the Hebrews were pushed to trust "a little more" each time.

Text	The Progression of the Hebrews' Trust in God
Ex. 5:19–21; 6:6–9	
Ex. 7:19–21; 9:8–10	
Ex. 9:22–26, 33	
Ex. 10:12–15, 18–19	
Ex. 10:21–23	
Ex. 14:21–28	
Ex. 16:4–5, 22–26	
Ex. 17:10–13	

2. God says that he took the Hebrews into the desert to humble them, test them, and know what was in their hearts (Deuteronomy 8:2–5). The Hebrew word translated "test" in Deuteronomy 8:2 does not imply testing in the sense of "enticing to do wrong." It implies proving a person's quality by experience.

a. What was the desert like? (See Numbers 20:4 – 5; Deuteronomy 1:19; 8:15 – 18; Jeremiah 2:6.)

b. In what ways do you think life in the desert would reveal the quality of a person's character?

THE "VAST AND DREADFUL" DESERTS OF THE SINAI OFFERED MANY OPPORTUNITIES TO LEARN TO TRUST GOD THROUGH HARDSHIP AND DIFFICULTIES.

3. What hopes did God have for his relationship with his people and what he wanted to accomplish through them? (See Exodus 6:7; 19:3 - 6; 29:44 - 46; Deuteronomy 4:35; 7:7 - 9.)

    Would it be possible for God and his people to experience that kind of relationship if his people remained prideful, independent, and confident in their own strength and abilities? Why or why not?

    What did God want to change in the hearts of his people by compelling them to go into the desert where they would face such hardship? (See Leviticus 26:19 - 20, 40 - 42.)

    Because God wants you to learn to follow him, what might he have to do to break through your human pride?

    What insight does James 1:2 - 4 add to your understanding of the benefit of "desert testing" — for us as well as for the Hebrews?

THINK ABOUT IT

Few people look forward to being trained in the desert. Exodus 15:22, in the Hebrew, literally says that Moses "caused, drove, made" Israel go into the desert. The Greek translation of Mark 1:12 records that the Spirit "sent" Jesus into the wilderness—exerting similar pressure on him. Yet the desert often is where God's people learn to trust him as their Shepherd and follow him faithfully.

4. Even after the Hebrews left the desert and entered the Promised Land, what did God continue to do — and why did he do it? (See Deuteronomy 13:1 - 4.)

FOR GREATER UNDERSTANDING

The three "lands" or geographical regions in which the story of the exodus and the wilderness wandering of the Hebrews takes place are Egypt, the desert, and the Promised Land (Canaan). Each of these can be viewed as metaphors for trust—God's primary lesson of the exodus.

- **Egypt** (Hebrew: *mitzrayim*) literally means "bondage." It was, in a sense, "Pharaoh's land." Here, all residents were to trust in Pharaoh. The Hebrews evidently came to believe (wrongly) that Pharaoh provided security, fertility, food, protection, guidance, and moral standards.
- **Wilderness** (Hebrew: *dabar*) also means "word" or "lead." This was God's land, the land he used to test and train his people. Here God provided food, water, safety, security, guidance, and moral standards to the Hebrews. The cloud, water from the rock, manna, the defeat of Amalek, and the Ten Commandments are all examples of God's provision for his people.
- **Canaan** (the Promised Land; Israel) was the land God gave to his ancient people. It was, in a sense, given to them to use in obedience to God. Here

continued on next page . . .

God desired that they continue to trust him as they had in the desert. He demanded that they reject Egypt — its worldview, all of its gods — as they did after he led them out of bondage. But once in Canaan, would God's people depend on him to provide moral standards, food, water, shelter, and protection? Or, would they trust once again in their own strength and the gods of neighboring cultures?

These three lands summarize, in a sense, the plot of the Hebrews' early history or "story." Yet it is also the plot of our story. If we have expressed a personal faith in God through Jesus, we also have been freed from sin's bondage. After God leads us into hard and difficult deserts in order to test and train us to totally depend on him, he blesses us and desires that we continually trust him for everything we need.

Reflection

God led the Hebrews into the desert, where for forty years they learned to trust him completely. In the Hebrew Bible, "desert" is used as a metaphor for times when life's journey is difficult and painful. Just as the Israelites had to learn to trust God and to follow him faithfully in the desert heat when they had no water, food, or shade, we must trust him and obediently follow him when the pain and suffering we face threatens to overwhelm us.

The apostle Paul, a great leader of God's people, also faced difficulties that threatened to overwhelm him. He wrote about one such experience in 2 Corinthians 12:7 – 10. In light of what you have learned about the Israelites' desert experiences and what God was accomplishing through them, take a fresh look at Paul's account:

> *To keep me from becoming conceited because of these surpassingly great revelations, there was given me a thorn in my flesh, a messenger of Satan, to torment me. Three times I pleaded with the Lord to take it away from me. But he said to me, "My grace is sufficient for you, for my power is made perfect in weakness." Therefore I will boast all the more gladly about my weaknesses, so that Christ's power may rest on me. That is why, for Christ's sake, I delight in weaknesses, in insults, in*

hardships, in persecutions, in difficulties. For when I am weak, then I am strong.

What had this difficulty caused Paul to recognize about himself in relationship to being humble before God?

Do you think Paul struggled to trust God rather than himself? Why, or why not?

To whom did Paul turn for help, and is this what God wanted him to do?

What does Paul seem to have learned about trusting in God's provision for him?

Think of one difficult "desert" experience God has used to shape you into being an obedient and godly person, as he did with Moses, the Israelites, and Paul. Describe what that was like and the spiritual lessons that you learned in the process.

During their years in the desert, God's people learned that God could and would provide just enough shade, water, and food at exactly the right moment if they would but follow his leading. What are you learning about trusting in God's provision for you?

Memorize

*Trust in the L*ORD *and do good; dwell in the land and enjoy safe pasture.*
*Delight yourself in the L*ORD *and he will give you the desires of your heart.*
*Commit your way to the L*ORD; *trust in him and he will do this:*
He will make your righteousness shine like the dawn, the justice of your cause like the noonday sun.

Psalm 37:3 – 6

Day Five | The Shepherd Who Would Come After Moses

The Very Words of God

But you, Bethlehem, in the land of Judah, are by no means least among the rulers of Judah; for out of you will come a ruler who will be the shepherd of my people Israel.

Matthew 2:6

Bible Discovery

Moses: A Great Shepherd, but Not Perfect

Moses, the Egyptian prince turned nomadic shepherd, matured to become a great godly leader. He developed an intimate relationship with God, and patiently, lovingly led the Hebrews as they struggled free from their bondage to Egypt and its ways. Although Moses stands out in biblical history as a leader like no other, he still was sinful and could not remove or pardon the Israelites' sins, much less the sins of all humankind. God would later send the Messiah — the sinless Shepherd — to give the ultimate sacrifice.

1. While it is accurate to say that Moses was the godly shepherd God chose to lead his people out of Egypt, there is so much more that can be said about this remarkable man. What sets him apart as a great man of God? (See Exodus

34:29–30; Numbers 12:3–8; Deuteronomy 34:10–12; Jeremiah 15:1; Matthew 17:1–3.)

2. Despite all of his strengths and accomplishments, not the least of which was shaping the Hebrews to be more like God, Moses remained a human being flawed by sin. In what way did Moses disobey God, and what were the consequences of that action? (See Numbers 20:8–12; Deuteronomy 34:4.)

What was it about Moses' action that was such a great offense against God?

Do you think God still considered Moses to be a successful "shepherd" of his "flock"? Why, or why not?

3. What did Moses say about the prophet who would come after him (Deuteronomy 18:15, 17–19), and what impact did those words still have on people during Jesus' time? (See Luke 7:16; John 1:21, 25; 6:14; 7:40.)

4. What metaphor did Jesus use to describe himself, and to what extent did it also describe Moses? (See John 10:11 - 16.)

   What set Jesus the Messiah apart from all other shepherd leaders, including Moses? (See John 1:17; Hebrews 3:3 - 6.)

   Why was it necessary for Jesus to come to earth? (See Acts 13:38 - 39; Romans 10:5 - 13.)

5. Shepherds lead and teach by speaking the word and being an example of the word. What is the relationship between Moses, who taught the Hebrews to live by the word of God, and Jesus the Messiah? (See John 1:1 - 14.)

6. In Deuteronomy 8:2 - 3, Moses told the Israelites, "Remember how the LORD your God led you ... to teach you that man does not live on bread alone but on every word that comes from the mouth of the LORD." To what extent did Jesus also live by these words and teach them to others in his speech and action? (See Matthew 13:1 - 9, 13 - 23; Luke 4:18 - 21; 5:1; 8:21; 11:28; 19:45 - 46; 24:27, 44 - 45.)

PROFILE OF TWO SHEPHERDS

Moses—The Godly Prophet and Shepherd Leader	Jesus—The Son of God and Good Shepherd
God protected baby Moses (Ex. 1:15–16; 2:1–10)	God protected baby Jesus (Matt. 2:14–15)
Had confrontations with evil (Ex. 7:10–12)	Was tempted by Satan (Matt. 4:1–11)
Fasted forty days in the desert (Ex. 34:28)	Fasted forty days in the desert (Matt. 4:2)
Controlled the Red Sea by God's command (Ex. 14:21–22)	Controlled the Sea of Galilee (Matt. 8:23–26)
Was the shepherd of God's flock, the Hebrews (Ex. 3:1–10)	Is the Shepherd who still leads his people—the body of believers, the church (Matt. 2:6; John 10:11–16)
Fed the Hebrews miraculously (Ex. 16:13–18)	Fed crowds of people miraculously (Matt. 14:13–21; 15:32–38)
His face shown with God's glory (Ex. 34:29–35)	His face shown with God's glory on the mountain (Matt. 17:1–2)
People grumbled against him at Marah (Ex. 15:24)	People grumbled at him (Mark 14:3–5; John 6:54–61)
His brother and sister spoke against him (Num. 12:1)	His brothers did not believe in him (John 7:5)
Interceded for the Hebrews (Ex. 32:30–33)	Interceded for his disciples and all believers (John 17:6–26)
Offered to atone for the sins of the Hebrews (Ex. 32:30)	Made atonement for the sins of humankind (Heb. 2:17)
Humbly "wrestled" with God in prayer concerning the Hebrews' complaints (Num. 11:1, 11–15)	Jesus, in a sense, "wrestled" with his Father in Gethsemane (Matt. 26:39; Mark 14:32–35)
God, through Moses, established Passover (Exodus 12:12–14)	Established communion to remember his bodily sacrifice (Luke 22:19)
Called the Word from God "life" (Deut. 32:46–47)	As the Son of God, is life (John 14:6)
Taught people to live by every word that comes from the mouth of God (Deut. 8:3)	Jesus is the Word (John 1:1, 14); Jesus quoted Deut. 8:3; he taught people to be servants of the Word (Luke 1:2)
Knew in advance when and where he would die (Deut. 32:50)	Knew in advance when and where he would die—the cross (Matt. 16:21)
Appeared after his death (Matt. 17:1–3) and spoke to Jesus and Elijah	Appeared after his death and spoke to many people (Luke 24:13–49)

Reflection

Great leaders lead by example, and Moses and Jesus did this powerfully. Moses taught people about God and showed them how to obey him. Jesus taught people about God and by his own example showed them how to live. Numerous passages in Scripture emphasize that those who claim to follow Jesus are to follow his example or, as 1 John 2:6 says, "walk as Jesus did." Jesus himself said that his "sheep" are to listen to his voice and follow him (John 10:27).

Who is the shepherd you follow, and whose voice do you listen to in your journey through life?

How closely have you observed the life and ministry of Jesus as recorded in the Gospels so that you can follow the example of the perfect and sinless Shepherd God sent to earth?

How greatly do you desire to be a follower of Jesus who thoroughly knows and faithfully applies God's Word?

How well are you living up to this commitment?

What improvements do you need to make?

To what extent do the people and leaders in your faith community pattern their lives after Moses and Jesus?

How would you go about doing this in your life?

BY EVERY WORD — STRIKING THE ROCK

Moses began his final official act as the leader of God's people with these words: "These are the words Moses spoke to all Israel in the desert east of the Jordan" (Deuteronomy 1:1). What follows is Moses' farewell address, or *devarim* (Hebrew for "words"). In this brilliant speech, Moses wove together the Israelites' history, the lessons of the desert, and the promise of the future if they would obey the words of their God.

No one had heard God's words more powerfully than Moses, to whom God spoke "face to face" as a friend. Often quoting God's words, Moses reminded the Israelites that the eternal words from the mouth of the Lord God — some of which they had heard with their own ears — were to be the foundation of their existence. Their identity and future were not based on their strength or even the Promised Land that they would soon enter. Rather, they would remain blessed if they never lost God's "words" that had been so powerfully heard and painfully learned in the desert. Their future as God's people depended on their hearing, believing, and obeying the words God had already spoken to them. Loss of power and land would not destroy Israel, but the loss of God's spoken words certainly would.

Moses challenged the Israelites to remember that the Torah — their "marriage" contract with God — was based on the words God gave them. The power of God's word created — between heaven and earth, between God and his people — a partnership of bringing *shalom* (peace, order, harmony) to a sinful world in chaos. So they were to remember always how God led them in the desert in order to teach them that man lives on every word that comes from the mouth of God (Deuteronomy 8:3).

Moses applied these lessons powerfully. He reminded the Israelites that their rebellion led to forty years of desert wandering, but that they must never forget God's loving care for them during that time. He reminded them that God is faithful to his words, which will never fail. And he warned them that to forget God's words is to forget the God who spoke them. To disobey them is to disobey the Creator of the universe.

Moses knew how easy it was to forget to hear God's words and obey them. He had done that himself at Kadesh Barnea when he hit the rock instead of speaking to it. So he reminded the Israelites that when their sin brought the curses in God's words to bear, he would forgive them: "When all these blessings and curses I have set before you come upon you and you take them to heart wherever the LORD your God disperses you among the nations, and when you and your children return to the LORD your God and obey him with all your heart and with all your soul according to everything I command you today, then the LORD your God will restore your fortunes and have compassion on you" (Deuteronomy 30:1 – 3).

God will be faithful to his eternal Word! By his grace he sent a greater Moses, Jesus the Messiah, to speak the eternal words of God, to live by every word that came from God's mouth, and to teach his followers to hear these words and put them into practice. The word of God was so focused in and through Jesus that it became his identity: "In the beginning was the Word, and the Word was with God, and the Word was God.... The Word became flesh and made his dwelling among us" (John 1:1, 14). That Word still gives life to people who live by every word that comes from the mouth of God!

Opening Thoughts (3 minutes)

The Very Words of God

> Then Moses went up to God, and the LORD called to him from the
> mountain and said, "This is what you are to say to the house of Jacob
> and what you are to tell the people of Israel: 'You yourselves have
> seen what I did to Egypt, and how I carried you on eagles' wings and
> brought you to myself. Now if you obey me fully and keep my covenant,
> then out of all nations you will be my treasured possession. Although
> the whole earth is mine, you will be for me a kingdom of priests and a
> holy nation.' These are the words you are to speak to the Israelites."
> So Moses went back and summoned the elders of the people and set
> before them all the words the LORD had commanded him to speak. The
> people all responded together, "We will do everything the LORD has said."
>
> *Exodus 19:3 – 8*

Think About It

Words are powerful. The right word spoken at the right time can
change a life or alter the course of history. Yet we sometimes under-
estimate the power of our words and use them carelessly.

How important and powerful do you believe God's words are? To
what extent is your professed belief evident in the way you respond
to God's words? In the way you talk with other people about God's
words?

DVD Notes (27 minutes)

God trains leaders to lead by the power of word

Miriam dies; water becomes a problem—again

God instructs Moses to *speak* to the rock

Severe consequences for Moses' disobedience

Be careful how you lead—remember the power of the word

Flawed but not a failure

DVD Discussion (7 minutes)

1. Using the map below, locate the Desert of Paran, where
    Israel wandered during their forty years of desert training.
    Next locate Kadesh Barnea. This is where Israel rebelled
    when the spies were sent into Canaan prior to their first
    attempt to enter the Promised Land. It is also where, forty
    years later, Moses hit the rock instead of speaking to it,
    which prevented him from entering the Promised Land.
    Now locate how far Egypt's influence had spread throughout
    this region — from Goshen to Serabit to Timnah and into
    Canaan.

    Consider the far-reaching influence of Pharaoh's "stick" — his
    physical and often cruel use of power. What insight does
    this give you into why God was so insistent that the leaders
    of his people be like shepherds who lead through the power

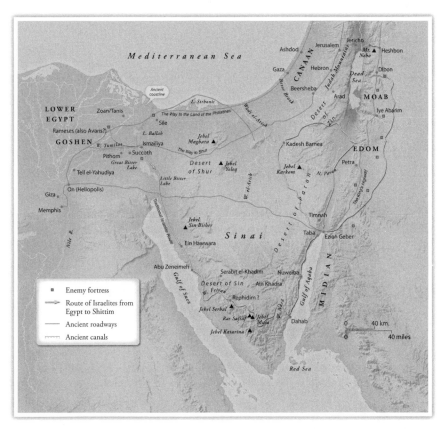

of his words, and not like Pharaoh who led with the brutal, physical power of his "stick"?

2. What do you think God wanted to accomplish when he allowed the water to run out at Kadesh Barnea just before the Israelites were ready to go into the Promised Land?

Did it surprise you that it happened at that place and time? Why or why not?

Do you think the Israelites viewed this hardship as one more test, one more opportunity to hear and follow their God? Why or why not?

How do you think Moses viewed it, and why?

3. What new information did you learn from the video about the story of Moses striking the rock at Kadesh Barnea instead of speaking to it?

How does what you have learned change your understanding of the story?

4. Many people have puzzled over why God disciplined Moses so harshly for hitting the rock instead of speaking to it. What did you learn from the video that gave you greater insight into the heart of God and a better understanding of his response to this situation?

5. What message about leadership in God's kingdom most impressed you from this story?

Whether or not you consider yourself to be a leader, how will you allow that message to impact your life, your relationship with God, and your relationships with his people?

Small Group Bible Discovery and Discussion (17 minutes)

Why the Desert?

The desert into which God led his people is harsh. Life is difficult, even for the few nomads who live there today. Without supplies from outside the desert, few would survive. In this desolate, virtually lifeless land, God revealed to the Israelites something more incredible than the pyramids, more lasting than the temples at Karnak, and more influential than the Pharaohs of Egypt: he spoke and gave them his life-giving words. Despite its hardships, the desert was not a place of punishment. It was a place of training where his people could hear his voice and learn to trust him fully.

1. Long before the Hebrews left Egypt, God had spoken to a few of their ancestors. The following passages record some of their interactions: Noah (Genesis 6:9 – 14); Abraham (Genesis 17:1 – 9; 18:16 – 33; 22:1 – 3, 9 – 12); Jacob (Genesis 28:10 – 17; 32:24 – 30). As you read these accounts, notice the kind of message God gave or the kind of conversation he had. Take note of the location or other circumstances surrounding his appearance.

    a. Of all the people God could have spoken to, why do you think he chose to speak to these people?

    b. In what ways do these interactions remind you of some conversations that took place between God and Moses?

    c. What hints do these accounts give you about what God wanted to say to the Israelites, and why he chose to speak to them in the desert?

    d. What do you learn from these interactions about the kind of relationship God longs to have with his people?

2. Deuteronomy 8:2–3 is a pivotal passage for understanding what God wanted the years of desert training to accomplish in the hearts and lives of his people: "Remember how the LORD your God led you all the way in the desert these forty years, to humble you and to test you in order to know what was in your heart, whether or not you would keep his commands. He humbled you, causing you to hunger and then feeding you with manna, which neither you nor your fathers had known, to teach you that man does not live on bread alone but on every word that comes from the mouth of the LORD."

   a. To what lengths did God go to silence the cultural "noise" of Egypt that had hindered his people from hearing him speak?

   b. What did he want to teach them, and how would life in the desert make God's purpose more significant to them?

POINT TO PONDER

Rabbi Lawrence Kushner has written that the wilderness is not just a desert through which God's people wandered for forty years. It is a way of being, a place that demands that we be present with all of ourselves. In the wilderness, we each are left alone each day with an immediacy that astonishes, chastens, and exults. We see the world as if for the first time.[1] In the desert, the noise of pleasant life in Egypt — whatever that is for each of us — grows increasingly faint, and God's voice becomes increasingly clear.

3. How did God impress upon his people the central importance of his words — not just for themselves, but for future generations? (See Deuteronomy 4:10 – 13, 32 – 36; 11:18 – 21.)

4. When people stop to be still before God, what can happen in their relationship with him? (See Exodus 14:14; Psalms 37:7; 46:10 – 11; Habakkuk 2:20.)

5. How important is it to God that his people listen to him and take his words to heart? (See Isaiah 51:1; 55:2 – 3; Jeremiah 26:2 – 6.)

OBSERVATIONS IN THE DESERT
A Reflection from Ray Vander Laan

There is a rabbinic saying, "The deeper you go into the desert, the closer you are to God." At first I thought that saying was just a reflection of the biblical story of God's people. I no longer think that is true.

Although I have been in the desert often, I am amazed each time by how still and quiet it is. Blowing wind against the rocks makes a distant sound. Otherwise I rarely hear anything. At first the silence seems uncomfortable, and I find myself listening for and even making sounds. Then I find that the stillness becomes a spiritual experience in which I become increasingly sensitive to myself and eventually to the reality of God's great power in the universe.

I now think that I understand why God told Moses to tell the Hebrews they were going three days' travel into the desert. I understand why God spoke

IMAGINE THE STILLNESS OF THE ISOLATED, WINDSWEPT LAND OF THE SINAI DESERT.

to them at Sinai, about forty days into the deep desert. It makes sense to me that followers of Jesus have often gone into the desert to seek a deeper relationship with him. Many people I have led into the deserts of the Middle East during the last thirty years have been deeply moved by the experience. The intense awareness of being alive and of God's presence has a profound impact. Such experiences begin with the overwhelming silence that greets those who enter the wilderness.

Thousands of years ago, God led his people out of Egypt's noisy culture — not literally like ours today, but loud nevertheless. A busy and complex lifestyle with all its activities and pleasures dulls the senses to self and certainly to God. Desert silence, however, makes it possible to once again listen to the voice of God. Perhaps that is why God still brings his people into the silence of challenging "desert" times. God wants to be heard, and he loves us enough to take us into the desert so that we can hear him speak.

Faith Lesson (5 minutes)

Many of us find it difficult to hear God speak because we rarely experience silence and do not set aside time to hear him reveal his words to us. Literally, we hear traffic, television, radio, people talking, elevator music, cell phones ringing. Metaphorically, jobs, families, hobbies, and friends grasp our attention, making it difficult for us to focus on God and *hear* his voice — listen, learn, and obey his words.

1. In Psalm 46:10, God commands: "Be still, and know that I am God." When was the last time you did this? Make sure you set aside time during the coming week to "be still." To begin, consider the following:

    a. Think about the great lengths to which God went in order to cancel the cultural "noise" that had hindered his people from hearing (obeying) his words. What effects might the literal and metaphorical "noises" in your life be having on your ability to hear and obey God's words?

    b. What does "stillness" look like in your culture, and how do you cultivate it in your life?

    c. Where might you need to go in order to find some "desert silence" so that you can hear God's words more clearly?

    d. When you *know* that God is God, how does that influence your life — your thoughts, words, and actions?

2. Are God's words important enough to you that you would ask him to give you a "desert," so that they become as significant in your life as they did for the Israelites in the desert? Why or why not?

Closing (1 minute)

Read Deuteronomy 8:3 aloud together: "He humbled you, causing you to hunger and then feeding you with manna, which neither you nor your fathers had known, to teach you that man does not live on bread alone but on every word that comes from the mouth of the LORD."

Then pray, asking God to open your eyes to whatever "noise" keeps you from hearing his voice and living by his words. Tell him of your desire to "feast" on the words from his mouth and your willingness to be humbled in whatever "desert" is necessary to teach you to hear his voice.

Memorize

He humbled you, causing you to hunger and then feeding you with manna, which neither you nor your fathers had known, to teach you that man does not live on bread alone but on every word that comes from the mouth of the LORD.

Deuteronomy 8:3

Learning to Live by the Word and Heart of God

In-Depth Personal Study Sessions

Day One | Changing the Hebrews' Perception of God

The Very Words of God

> *You saw no form of any kind the day the* L ORD *spoke to you at Horeb out of the fire. Therefore watch yourselves very carefully, so that you do not become corrupt and make for yourselves an idol, an image of any shape, whether formed like a man or a woman, or like any animal on earth or any bird that flies in the air, or like any creature that moves along the ground or any fish in the waters below. And when you look up to the sky and see the sun, the moon and the stars — all the heavenly array — do not be enticed into bowing down to them and worshiping things the* L ORD *your God has apportioned to all the nations under heaven. But as for you, the* L ORD *took you and brought you out of the iron-smelting furnace, out of Egypt, to be the people of his inheritance, as you now are.*
>
> *Deuteronomy 4:15 – 20*

Bible Discovery

The "Gods" that Are Seen vs. the God Who Is Heard

In ancient cultures, people often believed that the natural phenomena they could see — stars, moon, sun, rivers, sea, sky, animals, birds, fish, reptiles, plants — were either divine or represented certain deities. In contrast, the God of the Bible created all of these things. As such, he was separate from nature and demanded that his people *never* use the visual form of any created thing to represent him.

The Hebrews, however, came out of Egypt, where the people knew their gods through the visual "language" of obelisks, pyramids, temples, and gigantic statues. It would take a radical transformation for the Hebrews to know their God who revealed himself through the spoken word. What did God do at Sinai to help them experience him with their ears instead of their eyes?

1. When the Israelites arrived at Mount Sinai, they had seen the power of the God of their ancestors demonstrated in the plagues and in his provision for them on their journey. But the memories of Egypt's great temples and images of their gods remained fresh in their minds. What astonishing revelation of his presence did God provide at Mount Sinai? (See Exodus 19:1 – 22; 20:18 – 20.)

   What impressive visual phenomena were part of this experience?

   What did God do that was new to them, completely unheard of among the gods of Egypt?

   How do you think this intense sensory experience impressed God's people and influenced their growing understanding of him?

   Why do you think God was concerned that his people would try to come up to see him?

THE ARTIST'S IMAGINATION CAPTURES THE SCENE OF GOD SPEAKING TO HIS PEOPLE AT MOUNT SINAI. ALTHOUGH THE VISUAL PHENOMENA ASSOCIATED WITH HIS PRESENCE WERE IMPRESSIVE, THEY WERE NOT GOD. GOD DID NOT TAKE ON THE FORM OF ANYTHING THEY COULD SEE.

2. The events on Mount Sinai initiated a transformation in the Israelites' perception of God and their understanding of how to worship him. Unlike the gods of Egypt, their God was to be heard, not seen. In order to help them understand God's message at Mount Sinai, Moses cautioned the Israelites to be very careful about two things.

   a. What did he tell them to remember about that day? (See Deuteronomy 4:9 – 14.)

   b. What did he tell them never to do, and why? (See Deuteronomy 4:15 – 20.)

3. Which of God's commands shaped how the Israelites would know (experience) him? (See Exodus 20:1 – 4; 34:17; Deuteronomy 4:23 – 24; 5:4 – 10, 22.)

How different would the Israelites' experience of God be from that of the visual gods of other nations, and why? (See Psalm 115:2 – 8.)

What would be the consequences if Israel disobeyed this command? (See Deuteronomy 4:25 – 29.)

THINK ABOUT IT
Learning to Worship the Creator, Not the Creation

Mention the word "Egypt" and amazing images come to mind. Like all ancient civilizations, Egypt was a culture of the eyes. The green fertility of the Nile Delta, massive pyramids, glorious temples and tombs highlighted in dazzling color, stunning statues, and obelisks that could be seen for miles provided a feast for the eyes. This visual splendor culminated in the physical images of Egyptian gods that deified every aspect of natural phenomenon: sun, stars, sea, Nile River, birds, insects, fish, and animals.

Egypt's gods were believed to be present wherever the images that people created for them were found. In contrast, the Hebrews worshiped the Creator God who cannot be seen. The vast universe is the work of his hand, and everything that is seen is the result of his spoken word. Thus no biblical commandment is repeated more often than the prohibition against idolatry. Nothing awakens God's anger more than making and worshiping an idol, a mere image of something he has created.

4. What did Moses say to encourage the Hebrews — who had just come out of a culture that identified with hundreds of visual deities — to be confident and secure in their identity as the people of the one and only invisible God? (See Deuteronomy 4:5 - 8, 32 - 40.)

    Which actions and characteristics of God would make him real, present, and important to the Israelites?

    Which actions of the Israelites would make God real and present with them?

    How important were God's words becoming to the Israelites' identity?

PROFILE OF A CULTURE
The Visible Deities of Egypt vs. the Unseen God

Ancient Egyptians worshiped hundreds of deities. Often multiple deities were connected to a single, natural occurrence such as the annual flooding of the Nile, fruitfulness of the harvest, or childbirth. In addition, some natural phenomena were considered to be divine (e.g., the sun — Re) or to represent deities (e.g., the falcon — Horus).

According to Egyptian myth, whatever great gods such as Atum and Khnum brought into existence was deified. In contrast, whatever the one, unseen God of the Hebrews created was not a deity but an expression of his creative power. Because of the connection between Egyptian deities and creation, the gods were portrayed visually—often as a combination of human and animal or bird or fish or amphibian forms—and they (or what they represented) could be seen everywhere. For example, the Nile was the blood of Osiris. Hathor was portrayed as a cow. The scarab beetle represented Khepri, the rising sun. Mut was the vulture-headed goddess. The crocodile represented Sobek, the god of water and fertility. Carved onto walls of temples, palaces, tombs, and other man-made (and sometimes natural) structures, these voiceless images created a compelling sense of the gods' character and reality.

THIS CARVING ON THE WALL OF THE TEMPLE OF AMUN RE IN KARNAK ILLUSTRATES THE EGYPTIAN PRACTICE OF REPRESENTING DEITIES VISUALLY AS PARTLY HUMAN AND PARTLY ANIMAL, BIRD, OR SOME OTHER NATURAL PHENOMENON. ON THE LEFT IS THE LION-HEADED GODDESS OF WAR, SAKHMET. ON THE RIGHT IS THE FALCON-HEADED SUN GOD, RE HARAKHTY. BOTH WERE SUPPOSEDLY PARTLY HUMAN AND PARTLY DIVINE.

During the years they spent in Egypt, many Hebrews became convinced of this worldview and thought of deity in visual terms. Perhaps this is why they were quick to ask Aaron to create an image of their god while Moses was

continued on next page . . .

out of sight on Mount Sinai. The golden calf highlights the gulf between the visual gods they knew in Egypt and the unseen God they did not yet know.

In stark contrast to the speechless figures of Egypt's gods, the God of the Hebrews created the universe by the words of his mouth. The power of his stunning, brilliant words would transform his people if they would seek to know him with their ears, not their eyes. As part of God's plan to take Egypt out of his people and train them as his own, he forbade all visualizations of him "in the form of anything in heaven above or on the earth beneath or in the waters below" (Exodus 20:4)

5. What awesome — even terrifying — sights and sounds did God use at Mount Sinai to create an awareness of his presence while remaining invisible and separate from such powerful sensory phenomena? (See Exodus 13:20 – 22; 19:9, 16 – 18; Leviticus 9:23 – 24; Deuteronomy 4:10 – 12.)

Why do you think the Hebrews were more frightened by hearing God than they were of all the other awesome signs of his presence?

What do you think God intended the awesome and terrifying phenomena that accompanied his words to produce in his people?

Reflection

Today, people who desire a relationship with God through Jesus Christ face challenges similar to those of the ancient Hebrews. The visible, clamoring "gods" of our culture promise ease of worship, comfort, excitement, power, and fulfillment of our deepest desires. But how will we hear the powerful, life-changing, eternal words of our unseen God in the midst of the visible "gods" that surround us? What will lead us to have awe and respect for the mighty God of history who gives us his eternal Word — the Bible — and life everlasting? What will feed within us a passionate desire to love God and obey his every word with all our heart, all our soul, and all our strength?

Do people in your culture tend to place more confidence in what can be seen than in God's revealed Word?

If so, how has this impacted your desire to know and experience God?

When you hear the Bible's words — the very words of God — in what ways do you "connect" with them, and how do you respond?

To what extent do you associate the words you read with the words that the ancient Israelites heard from the mouth of God on Mount Sinai?

To what extent do the words you read capture your attention and produce within you a reverence and awe for God and his revealed Word?

Do you think it is important for you to reclaim the sense of awe that the ancient Israelites experienced at Mount Sinai? Why or why not?

Thoughtfully read Romans 3:1 - 2, Hebrews 4:12, and 1 Peter 1:23 - 25. What do these passages reveal about God's words, how they have been preserved for you, and what they mean to your relationship with God?

In what way do these passages have a similar purpose as God's words spoken to the ancient Hebrews at Mount Sinai?

It is no less important for followers of Jesus today to live by and be shaped by *every* word that comes from the Lord than it was for the Israelites. What new commitment do you need to make in order to "hear" every word that God wants you to hear?

Memorize

For you have been born again, not of perishable seed, but of imperishable, through the living and enduring word of God. For, "All men are like grass, and all their glory is like the flowers of the field; the grass withers and the flowers fall, but the word of the Lord stands forever." And this is the word that was preached to you.

1 Peter 1:23 - 25

Day Two | Learning to Live by the Word

The Very Words of God

> *Fix these words of mine in your hearts and minds; tie them as symbols on your hands and bind them on your foreheads. Teach them to your children, talking about them when you sit at home and when you walk along the road, when you lie down and when you get up. Write them on the doorframes of your houses and on your gates, so that your days and the days of your children may be many in the land that the* Lord *swore to give your forefathers, as many as the days that the heavens are above the earth.*
>
> Deuteronomy 11:18 – 21

Bible Discovery

Following the Words of Their Shepherd

In the desert, far from the visual "noise" of Egypt's gods, the God of the Hebrews spoke his words to his people. Like a desert shepherd, he taught them to listen for his voice. He gave them the tablets with Ten Commandments (in Hebrew, "ten words") written on them with his own finger and commanded them to live by every word that came from his mouth. He also impressed on his people the importance of remembering his words and teaching them to their children to ensure that future generations would continue to live by them.

1. As God led his flock (the Israelites) to sanctuary and pasture in the desert, what did he begin training them to do? (See Deuteronomy 6:1 – 4.)

   What was his purpose in doing this?

   What did he desire for his flock?

FOR GREATER UNDERSTANDING

The Word in the Desert

In the desert's silence, the spoken word of God could be heard, and God used that opportunity to the fullest. The Torah includes more than fifty references to God's words, and in classic Eastern fashion, the inspired writer of the Torah linked *desert* and *word* by constantly using words having the same root.

The Hebrew word translated "word," *dabar*, has the letters *dbr* (דבר) and can also be translated "commandment," "answer," "promise," or "response." *Dabar* is also the root word for *midbar*, which means "desert." These word links help to strengthen the message that God chose to speak to his people in the desert.

For example, God led his flock, Israel, into the desert (*midbar*) to instruct (*dabbret)* them in the Ten Commandments (in Hebrew, *debar*, meaning "ten words") and to teach them to live on every word (*dabar*) that came from his mouth. Also, the Hebrew word translated "pasture," *dober*, is based on the root *dbr* and is drawn from the reality that the shepherd (the Hebrew root noun for "desert," *dabar*, also means "leader" or "shepherd") often lived in the desert rather than in the fertile, farmed areas. So God led his flock into the desert (*midbar*) pasture (*dober*) where he spoke (*dibber*) so Israel would receive and learn his words (*dabar*).[2] What new insight does this give you into how much God wanted his words to be heard and understood in the context of the desert?

2. Desert shepherds lead their flocks by voice and by word, and God chose to lead his people in the same way. He first spoke his words from Mount Sinai, but his people were going to move on toward the Promised Land. How would God continue to speak his words to his beloved people as they traveled in the desert? (See Exodus 25:22; Numbers 7:89; Deuteronomy 10:5.)

When God gave these instructions, what was he communicating about his presence with his people and the importance of the words he would speak to them?

PROFILE OF A CULTURE
God Transforms His People

When God led his people out of Egypt, out of a culture in which deities were seen and not heard, he transformed the very nature of their religious faith. He taught them that he does not exist in things that can be seen in nature because all of nature is his creation, the handiwork of his word. Rather, he reveals himself in words that can be heard.

SHEEP FOLLOWING THEIR SHEPHERD'S VOICE

God wanted his people to be people of his word, people who were shaped by what they heard with their ears rather than what they pursued with their eyes. So God chose to speak his words to them in the desert where silence, not sight, overwhelms and dominates.

Like a shepherd, God patiently, faithfully guided them in his ways by his voice. Thus he established their faith on his spoken words and commanded them to teach future generations to also live by his words. As they heard God's words and gave them a place in their hearts and minds, the Israelites slowly but surely became people of the word.

3. In order to emphasize how seriously God took his command
    to live by his words, what did he tell the Israelites to do?
    (See Deuteronomy 6:4 – 9; 11:18 – 21.)

What do you think would be the impact of surrounding so
much of life by the words of God?

DID YOU KNOW?
Shema

God's command to Israel to hear his words (commands) in Deuteronomy
6:4–5 became known as the *Shema*: "Hear, O Israel: The LORD our God,
the LORD is one. Love the LORD your God with all your heart and with all your
soul and with all your strength." These words have been known by and have
shaped God's people ever since. When asked which is the greatest commandment, Jesus didn't use his own words to summarize the Torah; he
quoted the *Shema*.

To pray the *Shema* is to be reminded of one's commitment to love God, follow
him, and do his will. It is a way of placing God as king over one's life. Even
today, devout Jews pray the *Shema* morning and evening, and some Jewish
children learn the *Shema* as soon as they can talk. For a Jewish person, it is
the central affirmation of his or her commitment to the Lord.[3]

שמע ישראל

יהוה אלהינו

יהוה אחד

ואהבת את יהוה אלהיך

בכל-לבבך

ובכל-נפשך

ובכל-מאדך

Why was it essential that the Israelites do this for their children?

4. After spending forty years teaching the Israelites how to live on every word that came from his mouth, what did God tell them to wear, and why? (See Numbers 15:37 – 41; Deuteronomy 22:12.)

POINT TO PONDER

People of ancient cultures decorated their garments to show their identity and social status. The hem and tassels of the outer robe were particularly significant in conveying this symbolism. In fact, the corner of the hem would be pressed into clay to leave a person's official seal.

The tassels (*tsitsit*) Moses instructed the Israelites to sew on the hem of their garments served as a constant, visual reminder of the commandments — the words — God spoke at Mount Sinai (Numbers 15:37–41). By wearing tassels that included a blue thread, the Israelites were reminded of the priests' garments, and thus that they were God's treasured possession, a kingdom of priests and a holy nation whose mission was to display their God to the world (Exodus 19:5 – 6).[4] To wear this symbol as a community encouraged faithful obedience to God's every word.

Try to comprehend how important God's words are to him. He brought his people into the desert, spoke to them, wrote the summary words on stone, and commanded them to wear tassels on their clothes for all time — just so they would remember his words! For forty years, God taught his people how to "fix" his words in their hearts and minds and pass them on to future generations.

5. As his days on earth were coming to an end, Moses contin-
    ued to speak God's words to his people and prepare them
    for the Promised Land. To ensure that God's words would
    continue to be the formative influence in the lives of his
    people, what did God direct Moses to do, and what did he
    command all of Israel to do every seven years (Deuteronomy
    31:9 – 13)?

Reflection

God's words are as important today as they were during the time
of the exodus. They are as important for followers of Jesus as they
were for the Israelites. Our calling is like that of Israel: to learn to
live by God's every word so that we will be consistent witnesses
who display God's character in such a way that other people will
come to know him (1 Peter 2:9 – 12).

> To what extent do we, as individual Christians and as faith
> communities, still stand in awe of the amazing words God has
> spoken?

> To what extent have we kept the Word of God alive in our
> hearts?

Many religious Jews today have memorized significant portions
of their Scriptures and respond to the Word of God almost as if
they are standing at the foot of Mount Sinai — with reverence,
concentration, and joy. In contrast, how many followers of Jesus

have memorized large portions of the Bible or are deeply moved by hearing God's Word?

We know that God's Spirit lives within each person who follows Jesus (Ephesians 2:22; 1 John 4:12 – 15) and that other people "see" God through us.

Is it any less important for us to be shaped by God's words today than it was for the Israelites? Why or why not?

What are the consequences when followers of Jesus are not passionately faithful to God's words in all areas of life?

If God's words aren't essential to our lives or don't stir up a sense of awe and connection with God, we have some work to do.

What do God's words really mean to you?

Have you heard or read all of God's words — recently? Why or why not?

To what extent are God's words "fixed" in your heart, your mind, and your everyday life?

What are you willing to do to reclaim a more obedient walk with God that focuses on living by his every word?

Day Three | God's Leaders Keep Learning Too

The Very Words of God

> *Moses said to the* Lord, *"O* Lord, *I have never been eloquent, neither in the past nor since you have spoken to your servant. I am slow of speech and tongue."*
>
> *The* Lord *said to him, "Who gave man his mouth? Who makes him deaf or mute? Who gives him sight or makes him blind? Is it not I, the* Lord? *Now go; I will help you speak and will teach you what to say."*

Exodus 4:10 – 12

Bible Discovery

Moses, Miriam, and the Rock

Moses grew up in Pharaoh's household, led sheep in the desert, then became a great leader — God's chosen leader and spokesman — who led the Hebrews out of Egypt and into the Promised Land. Moses was a great and admirable leader, but he was far from perfect. Like the rest of us, he needed to learn to *hear* (obey) God's voice. He needed to learn to depend totally on God even when he felt unqualified or fearful. And he needed to keep learning so he would not lose sight of how God accomplishes his work through the words of his mouth and how tenderly he cares for his flock.

1. From the moment God assigned Moses his mission, he began training him in the importance of his word. In what way did God's communication differ from that of the gods Moses had known in Egypt? (See Exodus 3:4; Jeremiah 10:3 – 6.)

2. How did God instruct Moses to lead the Hebrews, and what role were God's words to have in that process? (See Exodus 3:13 - 15; 4:1 - 12.)

What concern did Moses have about speaking God's words, speaking on God's behalf, to other people? (See Exodus 3:13; 4:1.)

What signs did God provide to help Moses authenticate his message, and what impact do you think they had on Moses' experience of God? (See Exodus 4:2 - 9.)

What would be the main tool God would have Moses use to lead the Hebrews out of Egypt — the signs or his words? (See Exodus 4:10.)

What did God promise to do to help Moses accomplish the task God had given to him? (See Exodus 4:11 - 12.)

DID YOU KNOW?

Miriam and Aaron Keep Learning Too

Although Moses was God's chosen leader, he did not lead alone. Micah 6:4 records: "I sent Moses to lead you, also Aaron and Miriam." Because of Moses' fear or limitations in speaking, God sent Aaron, Moses' brother, to help him speak (Exodus 4:13–17). God also chose Miriam, a prophetess, to be a key leader of his people.

Apparently Miriam was a true woman of God in the tradition of Sarah, Deborah, Tamar, Ruth, Esther, and Mary. When she was still a child, she watched over the infant Moses hidden in the reeds at the edge of the Nile. When Pharaoh's daughter found the baby, Miriam arranged for his own mother to nurse him (Exodus 2:1–9). This alone was a significant contribution to the future of God's people. After the miraculous crossing at the Red Sea, Miriam took a tambourine and led all the women in a song of praise to God (Exodus 15:19–21).

Although Miriam served God for his glory, she had faults too. At one point, seemingly out of jealousy, she began to talk with Aaron against Moses (Numbers 12:2). Upon hearing her words, God had some teaching to do. He came down in a pillar of cloud to the Tent of Meeting and spoke to Aaron, Moses, and Miriam. When the cloud lifted, Miriam was leprous. For seven days she lived outside the camp. No Hebrews moved until she returned — healed and forgiven by God.

After that, Miriam seems to have carried out her role almost anonymously. In fact, when she died there is no mention that anyone mourned for her! In contrast, all of the Israelites mourned for Aaron for thirty days. According to Jewish tradition, one reason Moses became so angry with the Israelites at Kadesh Barnea (Numbers 20:10) was because of their failure to mourn for his beloved sister.

3. As he led the Israelites, Moses faced many challenges that shaped him in hearing and obeying God's words and in teaching God's people to do the same. Several of those challenges had to do with a crisis in the water supply, so consider what happened at Rephidim and Kadesh Barnea.

	Rephidim (Ex. 17:1–7)	Kadesh Barnea (Num. 20:1–13)
When the crisis occurred, how did the people treat Moses?		
What was the tone of their complaint, and against whom were they really complaining?		
Where did Moses turn for help?		
What did God tell Moses to do, and what about his instructions suggests that he wanted to teach his people through this response?		
Did Moses obey God's every word? What was the result?		
What message, what lesson connects with you and your commitment to hear and obey God?		

POINT TO PONDER

Consider the Possibilities

According to an ancient Jewish tradition, the Israelites had a rock in Egypt that provided water, and they took it with them when they went into the desert. So in instances when the Bible says Moses struck a rock that gushed water, it was the same rock each time and it provided water during much of their journey.

Although the Bible does not record this, there is some textual basis for this tradition. Israel seems to have had a constant source of water from a rock (Deuteronomy 8:15; Psalm 78:15–16; Isaiah 48:21). Furthermore, Paul appears to refer to this tradition (1 Corinthians 10:1–5) in making a connection between Jesus and the Hebrews of the desert journey. Whether the rock literally followed them or Paul drew on a fictional tradition, he makes the same point: Jesus is the ever-present sustenance of God.[5]

Another Jewish tradition holds that Miriam was responsible for the "water rock," or at least had suggested that they take the rock with them. It is interesting to note that there is no reference in the Torah regarding a lack of water from the time the Hebrews left Mount Sinai until Miriam's death (thirty-nine years!). Then, within days of her death, there are three occasions of thirst (Numbers 20:2, 19; 21:5).

Reflection

If someone asked, "How good are you at listening, knowing, and obeying the Word of God?" how might you respond? Most of us realize that we are too easily sidetracked by the "noise" of culture, spend too little time studying the Bible, and certainly fail in making obedience to God's words our top priority. We can take heart, however, in realizing that even Moses — who spoke with God face to face as a friend — needed to learn how to hear and obey God's voice. And even after forty years of intense training, he still could lose sight of what is most important and fall short.

What encouragement do you receive from Moses' life, particularly the fact that he needed years and lots of practical application in order to learn to hear and obey God's words — and lead other people?

How willing and eager are you to submit yourself to God's training in hearing and obeying God's words?

Do you think any follower of Jesus ever reaches the point when he or she hears and obeys God's voice always and completely? Why or why not?

Is it any less important to seek to do so with all your heart, soul, and might? Why or why not?

Which person(s) in your life has demonstrated for you what it is like to hear and obey God's voice, and what might you continue to learn from this person's example?

As you seek to lead and influence other people around you, why is it important to not only ask God to help you "speak" but to immerse yourself in the Word of God?

How does continual exposure to and intentional focus on God's words help you to obey him faithfully?

Try this: Using a computer search program, such as *Biblegateway .com*, look up all the references in which "word" and "Lord" are used in the same passage. Reflect on the central importance of God's word in his shaping of his people — then and now. Consider whether you are as aware of and obedient to the words of the Lord as he desires.

THINK ABOUT IT

When God appeared to Moses and revealed his deep concern for the suffering Hebrews, Moses at first insisted that he was not capable of God's assignment. He resisted the divine commission, finding new excuses that reflected the struggle and fear in his spirit.

Words were to be central to Moses' task of leading God's people, so he had to learn that God would use him despite his weaknesses. At the deepest level, this shepherd needed to learn to depend totally on God — and what better way to start learning this than for someone "slow of speech and tongue" to have a prominent role in speaking God's powerful words to Pharaoh and the Hebrews! From the start, Moses needed to depend, not on his knowledge, intellect, abilities, or experience, but on God's strength and God's words.

Sometimes God places us in situations for which we feel inadequate and unqualified. Like Moses, who needed to learn to hear and obey God's voice without question, we need to learn that God will be faithful to his every word. And we need to be faithful in listening to and obeying his every word — even when we think we know what to do.

Memorize

The LORD answered Moses, "Is the LORD's arm too short? You will now see whether or not what I say will come true for you."

Numbers 11:23

Day Four | Hear and Obey *Every* Command

The Very Words of God

> *The* Lord *said to Moses, "Take the staff, and you and your brother Aaron gather the assembly together. Speak to that rock before their eyes and it will pour out its water. You will bring water out of the rock for the community so they and their livestock can drink."*
>
> *Numbers 20:7 – 8*

Bible Discovery

Show Them the Power of the Word!

God and Moses had quite a relationship. In Exodus 33:11, we read, "The Lord would speak to Moses face to face, as a man speaks with his friend." From the time God spoke to Moses at the burning bush until the Israelites were poised to enter the Promised Land after forty years in the desert, God had spoken to and through this humble shepherd. As the leader of God's people, Moses was to speak God's words and reveal God's character, purpose, and power to his flock.

Again and again, Moses had spoken God's words and urged the Israelites to obey their God. Sometimes the people heard (and obeyed) these words; sometimes they did not. Moses saw the power of God unleashed when his people obeyed, and he saw the dire consequences of their disobedience. Despite all that Moses had seen and heard in his relationship with God and in his role as shepherd, he also had a moment when he failed to obey God's words.

1. After following God's voice for forty years and learning — fitfully at times — to live by every word that came from his mouth, what crisis did the Israelites face at Kadesh Barnea? (See Numbers 20:1 – 2.)

Although this generation of Israelites had heard God's words, experienced his shepherd leadership, and were poised to enter the land God had promised to their ancestors, what terrible things did they say to Moses (and to God) about their experience? (See Numbers 20:3 – 5.)

In what way(s) was their response similar to their ancestors' reaction during a similar crisis about forty years earlier? (See Exodus 17:3.)

2. How did Moses and Aaron respond to the people's anger, and what does this reveal about their commitment to lead by every word that came from the mouth of God? (See Numbers 20:6.)

3. When God told Moses what to do, what was he to take with him, what was he to do, and what would be the result? (See Numbers 20:7 – 8.)

Whose power and authority was symbolized by the shepherd's staff God told Moses to bring? (See Exodus 4:1 – 5; 7:14 – 21.)

In contrast to how God had instructed Moses many times in the past, what did God want Moses to use to convey his authority and power at Kadesh Barnea? (See Numbers 20:8.)

What do you think God wanted the Israelites to realize about him and the power of his words by seeing the spoken word bring water out of a rock?

4. Instead of obeying every word of God's command, as he had taught the Israelites to do, what did Moses do? (See Numbers 20:9 – 11.)

Why do you think Moses obeyed part of God's command, but not all of it?

What was really at stake here — in terms of understanding God and his desire for shepherd-like leadership? In terms of *hearing* (listening and obeying) God's words?

Instead of taking one more opportunity to show the Israelites the power of God's words, what kind of power did Moses demonstrate, and how do you think it may have impacted God's people?

FOR GREATER UNDERSTANDING
To *Hear* Is to Obey

God had taught the Israelites many lessons in the desert, a number of which are still being taught and modeled today. None is more central than God's desire for his people to live by every word that comes from his mouth (Deuteronomy 8:2–5) so that his words become the very foundation of their lives. Perhaps no lesson is harder to learn and practice than this one.

God led his people into the desert so that they would learn to live by his every word. At Mount Sinai and during their years of desert wandering, the Israelites heard God's words many times. But hearing and understanding God's words and *hearing* them are not the same thing. God wanted his people to learn the kind of hearing that becomes obeying.

Much as a parent might say to a child, "You'd better listen" because the child heard words but chose not to obey them, Moses had commanded the Israelites to *hear* God's words: "Hear, O Israel, and be careful to obey" (Deuteronomy 6:3). The Hebrew word translated "hear" or "listen" (e.g., Deuteronomy 5:1; 6:3–4) is *shema* (pronounced "shmah"). When translated into a Western language, it implies a physical action and a mental activity. Although many of us "hear," meaning that our ears pick up sounds, the Hebrew "hear," *shema*, means both physical hearing and the response to hearing — being obedient to what is spoken.

Reflection

When Jesus said, in Mark 12:29, "Hear, O Israel . . . ," did he mean, "Listen as a rational activity so you can recite and explain what I will teach you"? Or did he mean, "Obey"? When Jesus says "hear," he calls us to put his words into action, not just to listen to them. He wants us to be doers of the word, and not hearers only (James 1:22). So we can understand Jesus' statement "He who has ears, let him hear" (Matthew 13:9) as a call for obedience. As God's people, we have not truly heard God's words until we put what we hear into our hearts and allow these words to transform our lives.

God's words have power and purpose (Isaiah 55:10 – 11), especially when his people "hear" (obey) them.

What do you think God wanted to accomplish by having Moses speak to the rock?

When Moses failed to speak God's words to the rock at Kadesh Barnea, what opportunity do you think God's people lost?

Do you think God's people can ever let their guard down when it comes to learning to hear and obey God's every word? Why or why not?

As you look back on times in your life when you have not fully obeyed God's every word, what loss may you or others have suffered as a result of your disobedience?

What is your commitment today to be a faithful follower of God
and his Word, one who hears *and* obeys?

Memorize

> *As the rain and the snow come down from heaven, and do not return
> to it without watering the earth and making it bud and flourish, so
> that it yields seed for the sower and bread for the eater, so is my word
> that goes out from my mouth: It will not return to me empty, but will
> accomplish what I desire and achieve the purpose for which I sent it.*
>
> **Isaiah 55:10 – 11**

Day Five | Flawed but Not a Failure

The Very Words of God

> *So Moses took the staff from the LORD's presence, just as he commanded
> him. He and Aaron gathered the assembly together in front of the rock
> and Moses said to them, "Listen, you rebels, must we bring you water
> out of this rock?" Then Moses raised his arm and struck the rock twice
> with his staff. Water gushed out, and the community and their livestock
> drank.*
>
> **Numbers 20:9 – 11**

Bible Discovery

Moses Reverts to "Egypt Thinking"

During the years God led his people through the desert, Moses was
the unsurpassed example of *hearing* God's voice — listening to and
obeying the words of God. But even Moses had a moment of failure. At a crucial point in his leadership of God's people, he did not
"hear" God's instructions and rebelled against the power of God's
spoken word. Standing in front of the people to whom he had taught
and exemplified the importance of hearing and obeying God's word,
Moses had a great opportunity to demonstrate the power of God's
spoken word and add to their spiritual maturity. Instead, Moses

reverted back to the ways of Egypt and failed to care for God's flock and to honor God's words.

1. The Israelites had been to Kadesh Barnea before the account in Numbers 20 — forty years earlier.

    a. What serious sin did the Israelites commit the first time they were there, and what penalty did God impose? (See Numbers 13:1 - 20, 27 - 14:10; 14:20 - 23, 28 - 33.)

    b. What serious sin did Moses and Aaron commit the second time the Israelites were in Kadesh Barnea, and what penalty did God impose? (See Numbers 20:12.)

POINT TO PONDER
Did They Fail? Were They Failures?

When we think about how the Israelites responded to God, his promises, and his leaders after the twelve spies returned from Canaan, we tend to think that they were failures. In many ways, they did fail. But they also succeeded and were used by God in significant ways. They died in the desert, but during that time they trained their children in the ways of the Lord!

And Moses? There's no doubt that what he did at Kadesh Barnea was sinful and a disappointing failure for a leader of God's people who had walked with God so faithfully. But was he a failure? His sin against God cost him dearly, but his epitaph begins, "Since then, no prophet has risen in Israel like Moses, whom the LORD knew face to face" (Deuteronomy 34:10). Does this sound like the commendation of a failure?

Truly our God—the God of Moses, the God of Israel—is a God of redemption! Even to this day he is choosing human partners who, although we will fail, will join with him in his ongoing plan to restore *shalom* to his world.

2. Even when God's people sin against him and he must pun-
   ish them severely, God's loving, just, faithful, and forgiving
   character does not change. As you read the following Bible
   passages, notice how God described and/or responded to
   the sin of Moses and Aaron.

Text	God's Response to Moses' and Aaron's Sin
Num. 20:12–13	
Num. 20:23–30	
Num. 27:12–23	
Deut. 32:48–52	

3. Although one of Moses' last acts was sinful and cost him
   dearly, what does his epitaph reveal (in what it says and does
   not say) about God's forgiveness and desire to use his people
   to accomplish his purposes and bring about his kingdom?
   (See Deuteronomy 34:10 – 11.)

THINK ABOUT IT
Bible Heroes Are Flawed People Too

The Bible portrays its heroes with striking realism. They walked faithfully
before God with complete trust and obedience, great passion, and total self-
lessness in carrying out God's will. Abraham left his homeland after God's
call and later was willing to sacrifice his son. Rahab risked her life for the
Israelites because of her commitment to their God whom she barely knew.

Moses boldly spoke God's words to Pharaoh and the Hebrews. Young David bravely faced Goliath. Elijah stood alone as he demanded that God's people follow the Lord.

The Bible also realistically records the flaws and struggles of these same human servants. Abraham lied about Sarah, his wife, in order to save his life. Rahab was a prostitute. Moses, the unsurpassed example of someone who heard (listened and obeyed) the words of God, failed to obey God and hit the rock at Kadesh Barnea. David committed adultery and murder in his desire for Bathsheba. A despairing Elijah asked God to take his life.

Such stories, although they are painful, should also encourage us. As flawed people, we belong to the God who partners with sinful people to accomplish his purposes. He willingly chooses people with weaknesses, offers his healing forgiveness when they sin, and continues to use them as his witnesses. Their failures, and God's sometimes painful discipline, become God's words to future generations who also need to learn to live on every word that comes from the mouth of God.

Reflection

As a member of Pharaoh's family, and likely influenced by Pharaoh's leadership that was characterized by cruel displays of physical power, Moses struck (Hebrew: *vayakh*, "killed") an Egyptian who was mistreating a Hebrew (Exodus 2:11 – 15). At the time, Moses thought God was using him to rescue his own people. Although the Bible does not reveal if God approved or disapproved of Moses killing the Egyptian, God had a much different leadership training track in mind for Moses.

During the next forty years, the Egyptian prince learned to lead desert flocks by the words of his mouth, not by striking. And during the next forty years, he learned to lead the Israelites in the ways of God their Shepherd. Moses taught them to hear and obey God's words, teaching them to live by every word that came from God's mouth. He heard God's word, spoke God's word, and saw God's word accomplish unbelievable things as the Israelites learned to be the people God desired them to be. At Kadesh Barnea, however,

Moses reverted back to "Egypt's ways." Angrily calling the Hebrews "rebels," he struck (*vayakh*) the rock rather than patiently speaking the powerful words of God.

> Have you had instances in your walk of faith when you reverted back to sinful attitudes or behaviors that you thought you had left behind?

> If so, what were they, and what weakness or oversight in your walk with God may have led to them?

> What has been your experience in receiving God's forgiveness for these failures and restoring your relationship with him?

> Why do you think God caused water to come out of the rock to meet the needs of his people even after Moses *struck* it in disobedience?

> What encouragement do you find in this example of God's love for his people? His mercy for sinners?

Why do you think Moses' epitaph, written by God through the inspired writer, does not mention Moses' disobedience?

What encouragement does this give you to learn from your disobedience and persevere in learning to hear and obey God's every word?

What is your present commitment to hear and obey every word that comes from God's mouth, and what specific things do you do to keep focused on him?

Memorize

Hear, O Israel: The Lᴏʀᴅ our God, the Lᴏʀᴅ is one. Love the Lᴏʀᴅ your God with all your heart and with all your soul and with all your strength. These commandments that I give you today are to be upon your hearts. Impress them on your children. Talk about them when you sit at home and when you walk along the road, when you lie down and when you get up. Tie them as symbols on your hands and bind them on your foreheads. Write them on the doorframes of your houses and on your gates.

Deuteronomy 6:4 – 9

WITH ALL YOUR MIGHT: THE FINAL TEST

God delivered the Hebrew people from Egyptian bondage, but before they entered their long-promised homeland — a land "flowing with milk and honey" — they spent forty years in the "vast and dreadful" desert of Sinai (Deuteronomy 1:19). In this inhospitable desert, water is scarce; vegetation is sparse. Daytime heat can be nearly intolerable, and nighttime cold brings a deep chill. Travel is difficult because steep, rocky mountain ranges crisscross the landscape.

Yet in these desolate lands, God tested and disciplined his people. Over time he shaped and prepared them to become his holy nation, a kingdom of priests who would fulfill their mission of displaying his character to the world. In the desert God provided sustenance in the form of manna, water from the rock, and on occasion quail. He also provided spiritual sustenance, feeding his people on his words given in the Torah and portrayed through the tabernacle. In response, his people learned how to worship and obey their God and to live for him with all their heart, soul, and strength.

The desert training wasn't easy. The ways of Egypt had so thoroughly penetrated the hearts of the Israelites that they often disobeyed and rebelled against God. Eventually the generation that left Egypt as adults died in the desert, unprepared to take on the purpose God intended for them in the Promised Land. They did, however, rear a generation of children who trusted and obeyed the Lord and were ready to take on their God-given mission in the Promised Land.

As their wilderness journey ended, the Israelites began a new chapter in their history and in God's plan to reclaim his broken world. They would live in the land God had chosen for them — a beautiful, fertile land with springs and streams that would produce grain, fruit, and olives! God promised that they would lack nothing in this land. But would their years of desert training bear the fruit God intended? Would they still remember to obey and trust him completely, or would they gradually forget the lessons God so patiently taught them through the hardships of the desert?

Obedience to God's every word was and would always be essential to fulfilling their mission as God's holy nation. So Moses cautioned the Israelites to remember God and their covenant with him. In Deuteronomy, the last book of the Torah, which could be considered "the call to remember the God of the desert," Moses warned the Israelites:

> *When you have eaten and are satisfied, praise the LORD your God for the good land he has given you. Be careful that you do not forget the LORD your God, failing to observe his commands, his laws and his decrees that I am giving you this day.... Remember the LORD your God, for it is he who gives you the ability to produce wealth, and so confirms his covenant, which he swore to your forefathers, as it is today.*
>
> *Deuteronomy 8:10–11, 18*

Although this study will not delve into the life of God's people in the Promised Land, it is appropriate to conclude our study of the exodus in that land. The lessons learned through testing in the desert were to be lived out amidst the abundant blessings of the "good" land God provided for his people. But it can be difficult to remember those lessons when life is good. In fact, that proves to be the toughest test of all.

Like the Israelites, those of us who follow Jesus need to remember the lessons of the desert when God allows us to enjoy the blessings of a "good" land. Our training and God's blessings are for the purpose of bearing fruit and fulfilling our mission. Will we remember and be faithful to obey God's every word, or will we be tempted to forget and fail to produce the harvest?

Opening Thoughts (3 minutes)

The Very Words of God

> *Remember how the* LORD *your God led you all the way in the desert these forty years, to humble you and to test you.... He humbled you, causing you to hunger and then feeding you with manna ... to teach you that man does not live on bread alone but on every word that comes from the mouth of the* LORD.... *For the* LORD *your God is bringing you into a good land — a land with streams and pools of water, with springs flowing in the valleys and hills; a land with wheat and barley, vines and fig trees, pomegranates, olive oil and honey; a land where bread will not be scarce and you will lack nothing.*
>
> *Deuteronomy 8:2 – 3, 7 – 9*

Think About It

When we experience God's abundant provision, it is tempting to pursue more than we need or to credit ourselves rather than God for what we enjoy. Both of these are ways of not "remembering" God.

In what ways do people today, including people who claim to follow Jesus, fail to "remember" God — who he is, what he has done, and how he wants his people to obey his words and live fruitful, God-honoring lives?

DVD Notes (29 minutes)

Facing the toughest test of all

God's mission for Israel in the terraced farms of Judah

Be careful you do not forget your God

God builds a fertile hillside for his people

When God finds *be'ushim*

DVD Discussion (7 minutes)

1. Using the map below, locate the Judah Mountains where this video was filmed. The western slopes of these mountains, facing the Mediterranean Sea, receive the most rain and are suitable for terraced farming. Just a few miles to the east, however, the Judah Mountains receive far less rain and quickly become desert wilderness (the land of the shepherds) as the eastern slopes of the mountains drop off steeply toward the Dead Sea.

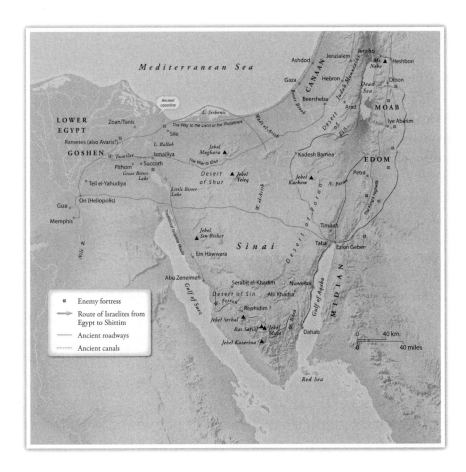

2. By the time they entered the Promised Land, the Israelites
    had spent most, if not all, of their lives as nomads in the des-
    ert. What do you think it was like for them to have homes in
    which to live and fertile ground to call their own?

    Do you think the opportunity to live such a blessed life
    would make you inclined to remember or to forget God and
    the lessons of the desert? Why?

**IMAGINE THE BLESSING THE PROMISED LAND'S *GANIM* PROVIDED IN
CONTRAST TO THE HARSH, BARREN DESERT WHERE THE ISRAELITES
HAD LIVED FOR A GENERATION.**

3. God wanted the Israelites to be a holy nation, a kingdom of priests who would live such holy lives that they would demonstrate the true character of God to the world. Imagine for a moment that you are a stranger traveling through the Promised Land. What might you think about the God of these righteous people who lived in harmony in the beautiful *ganim* (singular, *gan*) of the Judah Mountains?

   What might you think about the God who provided so abundantly for his people and whose people were honest, kind, generous, and just?

   In what ways might you think differently about the God of people who lived in the *ganim* as opposed to the God of people who lived in the desert?

4. When you consider the work it takes to build a *gan* — to remove the rocks, build the walls, prepare the soil, plant the vines, build the watchtowers — what understanding does it add to your picture of God's love, faithfulness, and commitment to his people and to his plan to restore *shalom* to his world?

5. To what extent has this video helped you to better understand the grief God's loving, passionate heart must feel when

his people fail the "test of prosperity," when they forget him
and produce a harvest of *be'ushim*?

Small Group Bible Discovery and Discussion (15 minutes)

The Land God Promised

Out of all the possible places God could have chosen as a homeland
for his people, he chose the land of Canaan, or Israel as it would
later be called. Why? Why did he promise *this* land to Abraham's
descendants? Although the Bible does not fully reveal the mind of
God in this instance, it does provide clues as to what God desired
of his people and how the nature of that land would continue to
shape them into the "kingdom of priests" and "holy nation" (Exodus
19:5 – 6) he desired them to become.

1. Imagine how beautiful the land of Israel would appear to
    people who had spent a lifetime in the desert! As you read
    the following passages, notice the phrases used to describe
    the fertile land God promised to give to the Israelites.

The Text	Phrases that Describe the Land
Gen. 13:14 – 18	
Ex. 3:8	
Deut. 6:10 – 12	
Deut. 8:7 – 9	
Deut. 11:11 – 12	

What is God's relationship to this land? (Hint, see Deuteronomy 11:11 – 12.)

What does the gift of this land reveal to you about the kind of life God wanted to provide for his people?

2. When God brought his people into the Promised Land, he was not just giving them land, he was giving them land that came with a relationship — a relationship with him! That relationship must have been extremely important to God because he spent forty years training and testing his people so that they would learn to obey his every word and, therefore, be prepared to enter the land and fulfill his purpose in it. According to the following texts, what did God require of the Israelites in terms of their relationship with him that would ensure their receiving the full benefits of their new land?

   Exodus 19:3 – 6; Deuteronomy 6:1 – 3, 13 – 19; 11:31 – 32

   Deuteronomy 6:10 – 12

   Deuteronomy 11:10 – 15

3. In what ways would the Israelites' commitment to maintaining an intimate relationship with God fulfill his purpose for them in the land? (See Exodus 19:5 - 6.)

Do you think faithful obedience and an intimate relationship with God is as essential to fulfilling God's purpose in the world today as it was when the Israelites lived in the Promised Land? Why or why not?

What have you learned about the Israelites' need to "remember" God and live in intimate relationship with him that relates to how God's people today experience their relationship with him and fulfill his purpose?

DID YOU KNOW?
A Land Flowing with Milk and Honey

The phrase "milk and honey" that is used to describe the land God promised to give to the Israelites, describes a land that is good for farmers as well as for shepherds. In the land of the Bible, milk primarily came from goats, not cows. So a land with "milk" would have pasture for the shepherds' flocks, a necessity that the herdsmen patriarchs—Abraham, Isaac, and Jacob— knew well.

The description of the land flowing with "honey" takes a bit more work to unpack. In Deuteronomy 8:7 – 10, God promised that the good land to which he would bring his people produced seven foods—wheat, barley, vines (grapes), figs, pomegranates, olive oil, and honey. All of these foods are plant products except honey, which is made by bees. A Jewish perspective suggests that "honey" mentioned in the Deuteronomy passage and in the "milk and honey" passages is a sweet syrup or jam made from fruit—particularly dates, for which the same Hebrew word, *devash*, is used.

A "land flowing with milk and honey" is an apt description of Israel's geography. It is a land where both shepherd and farmer can exist in peace and produce a rich harvest. The term also beautifully illustrates the biblical metaphors of shepherd and farmer that refer to God (and the Messiah, his Son) and his caring, nurturing relationship with his people (Psalm 23:1; Isaiah 5:7; John 10:14; 15:1).

THE PROMISED LAND WAS SUITED TO PROVIDE AN ABUNDANT HARVEST FOR THE SHEPHERD AND THE FARMER.

Faith Lesson (5 minutes)

God chose and prepared a land that was strategically located in which the Israelites could fulfill their mission as a holy nation, a kingdom of people committed to being like him so that the whole world would know — as David later proclaimed — "that there is a God in Israel" (1 Samuel 17:46). God chose and strategically trained his people for that role. Through the testing in the desert, they learned to obey and trust him. And amidst the blessings of the land God gave to them, they needed to remember and live by those lessons continually so that they would fulfill God's purpose. God is still in the business of preparing people — through hard times and times of blessing — to display his character to the world.

1. Why do you think it was crucial for the Israelites to learn the lessons of the desert *before* they entered the Promised Land and experienced its blessings?

    Do you tend to be more faithful in remembering God — obeying and depending on him — when you are experiencing hardship or when you are enjoying a time of blessing? Explain.

2. As you consider the experience of the Israelites in the desert and in the Promised Land, in what ways have you become more aware of the importance of your daily relationship with God — your dependence on his provision and need to obey him in every area of your life?

In what ways has your perspective on and response to difficult times of testing changed?

In what ways will you view and respond differently to times of blessing?

3. Where are you in your relationship with God right now? Are you in the desert learning? In the *ganim* remembering and depending on God? In the *ganim* feeling self-sufficient and ignoring God's role in your life? Or is your life producing *be'ushim*?

What would you like to change in your relationship with God, and what would it require you to do?

What is your commitment to making that change and cultivating your relationship with God?

FOR GREATER UNDERSTANDING
Depending on God in a Land "Flowing with Milk and Honey"

The Bible describes the Promised Land as a most beautiful land flowing with milk and honey (Ezekiel 20:6). But life there would never seem quite as secure as life in Mesopotamia (where Abraham came from) or in Egypt — lands where the great Tigris, Euphrates, and Nile rivers nearly always flooded fertile farmland and ensured a successful harvest.

In Egypt, the future harvest seemed relatively certain and predictable, like the stars and the seasons. How easy it would have been for the Hebrews to forget that God was the ultimate source of the Nile. How easy it would have been for them to believe that the work of their hands produced the harvest. Why would they have "looked up" toward heaven when they had such success tending the soil beneath their feet?

The Promised Land had great fertility, but its mountains and valleys were watered by rain, not by annual flooding or irrigation. No matter how hard the Israelites worked the rocky soil, their land would never produce anything unless God provided the rain at the right times. So there would be a clear distinction between the efforts of God's people, on one hand, and their faith and trust in God to provide for them.

Perhaps the biggest risk the Israelites faced in their new land lay in trusting in their abilities and achievements rather than depending on the provision of their faithful, sovereign God. Whether they lived in the desert or in the land of milk and honey, God wanted his people to trust him completely, obey his every word, and depend on him for everything. The land of Canaan would help to continue the process of shaping the minds and hearts of God's people that he began in the desert.

Closing (1 minute)

Read Deuteronomy 8:10 - 11, 18 aloud together: "When you have eaten and are satisfied, praise the LORD your God for the good land he has given you. Be careful that you do not forget the LORD your God, failing to observe his commands, his laws and his decrees that I am giving you this day. . . . Remember the LORD your God, for it is he who gives you the ability to produce wealth, and so confirms his covenant, which he swore to your forefathers, as it is today."

Then pray that God will remind you of your need to depend on him and receive his blessings with thankful hearts. Ask him to help you to become more obedient to his Word and sensitive to his leading, and to be more willing to share the blessings he has given you with other people.

Memorize

> *When you have eaten and are satisfied, praise the LORD your God for the good land he has given you. Be careful that you do not forget the LORD your God, failing to observe his commands, his laws and his decrees that I am giving you this day. . . . Remember the LORD your God, for it is he who gives you the ability to produce wealth, and so confirms his covenant, which he swore to your forefathers, as it is today.*
>
> *Deuteronomy 8:10 - 11, 18*

Learning to Live by the Word and Heart of God

In-Depth Personal Study Sessions

Day One | Why Did God Test His People?

The Very Words of God

> Remember how the LORD your God led you all the way in the desert
> these forty years, to humble you and to test you in order to know what
> was in your heart, whether or not you would keep his commands.
>
> **Deuteronomy 8:2**

Bible Discovery

Forty Years of Testing in the Desert

When God delivered the Hebrews from Egyptian bondage, they
proudly marched into the desert armed for battle (Exodus 13:18).
But their bold confidence quickly waned. Even after seeing God
destroy the Egyptian army at the Red Sea, the people whom God
selected to represent him to the world became afraid that the desert
would destroy them. They repeatedly grumbled and rebelled against
God, refusing to trust in his provision or to live by his words. Finally,
with just a few exceptions, God declared that no one twenty years
of age or older would enter the land promised to their ancestors
(Numbers 14:29 – 30). For the next forty years, God's people would
wander in the desert, learning to trust him and love (obey) him with
all their heart, soul, and strength.

1. What kind of picture does Scripture paint of the desert? (See
    Numbers 20:4 – 5; Deuteronomy 1:19; 32:10; Jeremiah 2:6.)

Why would a loving God want his people to live in such a place? (See Deuteronomy 8:5.)

Which metaphor did God use to describe his relationship with his people during this time, and in what ways did he demonstrate that depth of love for them? (See Deuteronomy 8:5; 32:10 – 12.)

DID YOU KNOW?
What Kind of "Testing" Did God Have in Mind?

The Hebrew word translated "test" in Deuteronomy 8:2 is *yada*, which means to know something experientially not just intellectually. It also conveys the idea of proving or testing the quality of someone by experience. So God tested the Israelites' hearts to discover and know their true character and quality, not to entice them to do wrong.

2. Before God appeared to his people at Mount Sinai, he gave Moses a message for the Israelites. After reminding them of what he had already done for them, what did he reveal about his purpose for them and how they were to accomplish it? (See Exodus 19:3 – 6.)

3. In Deuteronomy 8:2 – 3, at the end of their forty years of training in the desert, Moses again reminded the Israelites of what God had done for them and why. Read this passage

carefully and consider what you think God had wanted the Israelites to discover during their time of testing:

About themselves and their abilities

About himself

About obeying and keeping his commands

4. What insight do you gain from Proverbs 3:5 - 8 and Isaiah 31:1 into why God longs for his people to trust him — and only him — to fully meet their needs?

5. What did God warn would happen if the Israelites did not completely trust him and live by every word that came from his mouth? (See Deuteronomy 8:10 - 16.)

What similarities do you see between God's warning and the attitude of his people when they first left Egypt?

What did God really want for his people in the Promised Land, and what attitude would prevent them from receiving that blessing?

Reflection

In our self-sufficient, you-can-achieve-it, do-it-your-way culture, it is easy to take credit for the "good" things in life and ignore the fact that God has provided all that we have. It is hard for us to humble our proud hearts and view our lives as a response to God's Word, God's purpose, and God's provision. It seems that God's ancient people struggled with these same challenges, so God led them into the desert to train them to follow him.

As a result of facing trials and testing, what do you think the Israelites discovered about their God and their devotion to him?

As a result of learning about the Israelites' experiences, what have you discovered about God and your devotion to him?

In what ways did the Israelites' experiences lead them to trust God more fully?

In what ways have the trials and testing you have faced led you to trust God more fully?

When have you been tempted to depend on your strength or the strength of other people rather than on God?

How did you respond, and what was the result?

How might have you responded differently if you had been more serious about having a humble heart that seeks to live by every word that comes from God's mouth?

How would your attitude toward difficult circumstances change if you truly believed that God loves us enough to lead us into desert experiences in order to teach us to live by his every word so that life will go well for us?

Memorize

Consider it pure joy, my brothers, whenever you face trials of many kinds, because you know that the testing of your faith develops perseverance. Perseverance must finish its work so that you may be mature and complete, not lacking anything.... Blessed is the man who perseveres under trial, because when he has stood the test, he will receive the crown of life that God has promised to those who love him.

James 1:2 – 4, 12

Day Two | God Gave His People a Land to Possess

The Very Words of God

> *Hear now, O Israel, the decrees and laws I am about to teach you.*
> *Follow them so that you may live and may go in and take possession of*
> *the land that the LORD, the God of your fathers, is giving you.*

> **Deuteronomy 4:1**

Bible Discovery

The Israelites' Mission: To Be Like God in Their World

God redeemed his people to be his witness that he alone was God (Isaiah 43:1, 10 - 12). And he gave them a land in which they would be his holy nation, his kingdom of priests who would display his character to the world (Exodus 19:3 - 6). In order to possess the land God had chosen for them and to be his witnesses, the Israelites needed to remember the lessons God taught them in the desert. They needed to trust in his provision and obey his commands completely.

The Israelites' very existence in the Promised Land was a message. The way they lived would display God's character to the world. If they refused to obey God's commands and displayed a false picture of him, how could he let them continue to live in the land?

1. From the beginning of his relationships with humankind, it seems that God has made a connection between his people living well in the land he provides for them and their obedience to him. Consider, for example, the Garden of Eden.

    a. Why did God put people in the garden? (See Genesis 1:27 - 28; 2:8 - 15.)

    b. What prevented God's people from continuing to be his partners and fulfill their mission to increase, fill, and rule his world? (See Genesis 2:16 - 17; 3:11 - 13, 23 - 24.)

2. God's purpose for the Israelites was to join him in his ongoing plan to restore *shalom* to his chaos-stricken world. Their total obedience to him in the land he provided was essential to that plan.

    a. What did God want to happen when he gave the Promised Land to the Israelites? (See Deuteronomy 6:17 – 19; 8:1; 11:31 – 32; 16:20.)

    b. In light of God's purpose for the Israelites in the Promised Land and what happened in the Garden of Eden, what do you think could prevent the Israelites from continuing to be God's partners and fulfilling their mission in the Promised Land?

    c. What did God say repeatedly (more than 250 times!) about the connection between the land and his people's relationship with him, and what does this communicate to you about how important God considers the obedience of his people to be? (See Exodus 6:8; 19:5; Psalms 25:12 – 13; 37:29.)

FOR GREATER UNDERSTANDING
To "Possess" the Land

Many times God had promised to give Canaan as a *morashah* (typically translated as "possession" in English) to Israel. But the root of this word has a richer meaning than simply possession through legal ownership. In the Eastern world of the Bible, *morashah* is not a legal concept primarily, but expresses ownership that is confirmed by ongoing use of the land. The English word "heritage," which is used to translate Exodus 6:8 in the *King James Version* and the *New King James Version*, suggests this deeper meaning.

For Israel, two things were *morashah*—the Promised Land and the Torah (Deuteronomy 33:4). Just as the Torah is not something to be acquired but is to be "owned" or "possessed" through obedience, the land God chose was not simply to be gained through legal title but was to be "owned" or "possessed" by appropriate use. It was (and still is) a heritage, a gift from God that belonged to those people to whom it was given only when they used it exactly as he commanded.

Perhaps God chose the land of Canaan over all other lands because it demanded a lifestyle of obedience and dependence on God for rain. It would provide everything his people needed only if they followed his ways exactly while they lived in it and cared for it. Because the nature of the land itself demanded obedience to God in order for God's people to "inherit" it, they would be compelled to use the land to serve him.

3. What understanding do you gain from the following passages regarding the consequences of the Israelites' obedience (or disobedience) in the Promised Land?

Text	Positive Outcomes: God's Blessings	Negative Outcomes: God's Punishments
Lev. 26:1–20		
Deut. 7:12–15		
Deut. 11:8–17		
Deut. 28:1–24		

DID YOU REALIZE?

When the Israelites arrived in the Promised Land, each family received a plot of land as an eternal inheritance. On Mount Carmel, the gentle slopes of the Samaria Mountains, and the steep hillsides of the Judah and Hebron Mountains, this land was typically a *gan*, with little more than three or four olive trees, a fig tree, and a few vines.

THE BEAUTIFUL TERRACED HILLSIDES OF THE JUDAH MOUNTAINS PROVIDED FERTILE SOIL FOR A RICH HARVEST.

Long before the Israelites arrived in the land, the Canaanites had started building terraces on the slopes of the steep hillsides in order to expand available agricultural land. These terraces maximized available water, provided proper drainage, and became very fertile. As the Israelites became acquainted with the region — including its soil, climate, and water conditions — they turned more than 50 percent of the western slopes of the Judah Mountains into highly developed, fertile farms.[1] The Judah Mountains, covered by terraced *ganim*, thus became a metaphor of the kingdom of the Messiah to come (Micah 4:4).

Reflection

In Deuteronomy, Moses' last speech to the Israelites testified to the beautiful, fertile land that God would soon provide and through which he would demonstrate his love and faithfulness to them. What they may not have realized was that the land was not just a place where wheat and barley, olives, figs, and grapes grew in abundance due to God's blessing of rain. This land was also where God wanted to "plant" his people so that they would grow and produce abundant fruit for him. Although few of us live in that land today, the desire of God's heart for his people to grow and produce abundant fruit has not changed.

If you are a follower of Jesus, what has God given to you in your life that, like the Promised Land God gave to the Israelites, helps to display his character to people around you? (Hint: this might be a particular job, a relationship, or place.)

How are you using (or how might you use) whatever God has given you, like the Israelites used their *gans*, to give evidence of God in your everyday life?

In what ways is whatever God has given you also helping you to grow in your relationship with him and to produce spiritual fruit?

How would you describe the fruit that God wants your life to produce?

Based on the evidence of your life, which is to display God's character, what words might someone use to describe God?

What weaknesses do you see in your obedience to God, your dependence on him, or your thankfulness for his provision that are "stunting" your spiritual growth or displaying a false picture of God?

Which specific commands of God do you need to be more diligent in obeying to correct these failures?

Day Three | Just Enough

The Very Words of God

> *Then the Lᴏʀᴅ said to Moses, "I will rain down bread from heaven for you. The people are to go out each day and gather enough for that day. In this way I will test them and see whether they will follow my instructions." ... The Israelites ate manna forty years, until they came to a land that was settled; they ate manna until they reached the border of Canaan.*

Exodus 16:4, 35

Bible Discovery

Learning to Trust in God's Daily Provision

By the time the Israelites entered the Promised Land, which was a paradise compared to the desert, they had learned much about God and his provision. In the desert, God had carefully orchestrated their experiences so that they would learn to obey all of his commands and receive the blessings of his provision. Rather than allowing the Israelites to gather days or weeks of manna at one time, for example, he gave them enough for each *day*. Any manna they hoarded stank and became inedible. The exception, of course, was on the sixth day, when he instructed them to gather an extra portion to eat on the Sabbath. This was but one of the lessons that taught the Israelites to obey God's words, depend on his provision, and trust that he would provide enough for each day.

1. The Israelites who were entering the Promised Land had learned how to follow God's leading and trust him to provide just enough to survive each day — giving them just enough water (out of the rock) and just enough manna (from heaven), and guiding them to just enough grass on the desert hillsides to feed their flocks and herds. How did Moses describe God's daily provision for his people, and what do his words reveal about God's character and love for his people, and Moses' trust in God? (See Deuteronomy 2:7.)

Knowing that life in the Promised Land would be quite different from what the Israelites had experienced in the desert, what did Moses emphasize to the Israelites as they were poised to enter the Promised Land? (See Deuteronomy 8:6, 10 - 14.)

How is being satisfied with God's provision each day quite different from the mind-set of seeking self-gratification or the need to grasp for security by accumulating more than we need for each day?

2. The land God gave to the Israelites would provide abundance, but not excess. Through God's ongoing blessing, the land would provide just enough to satisfy the needs of his people, leading them to continue trusting in him to sustain them — just as they had during their years in the desert. What do the following passages reveal about God and his provision for those who remain faithful to him?

Text	What Is Revealed about God and His Provision?
Deut. 7:9	
Ps. 9:10	
Ps. 65:9 – 13	
Ps. 146:5 – 8	
Matt. 6:25 – 33	

From these brief examples of God and his provision for his people, do you think God takes pleasure in providing for his people? Why or why not?

Would you be willing to trust in a God who provides like this? Why or why not?

POINT TO PONDER
Learning to Depend on God for "Just Enough"

Some Western Bible readers are surprised to learn that the "green pastures" of Israel are seemingly barren hillsides in the wilderness. Tufts of grass, watered by small amounts of rainfall or dew, grow from between the rocks imbedded in the soil. If the flock follows the shepherd, each animal will have just enough grass to eat each day.

THIS TYPICAL SCENE IN THE NEGEV DESERT ILLUSTRATES THE SHEPHERD LEADING HER FLOCK TO JUST ENOUGH PASTURE TO MEET THE NEEDS OF THE DAY.

continued on next page . . .

Like a shepherd, God led his people through the wilderness, teaching them that if they trusted him and followed (obeyed) him, he would provide enough to meet their needs for that day. When he brought his people into the Promised Land, he wanted them to continue to depend on him. As his people enjoyed the beauty and fertility of the *ganim*, he wanted them to think of him and their relationship with him. He wanted his people to look to him to sustain them day by day as they obeyed his commands.

TO A HUMBLE HEART THAT DESIRES TO DEPEND ON GOD, THE *GAN* IS A BEAUTIFUL REMINDER THAT GOD WILL PROVIDE "JUST ENOUGH" AS HIS PEOPLE FOLLOW (OBEY) HIM.

Reflection

Solomon had the "good life" — more than enough in his vineyards, gardens, and parks; more than enough herds and flocks; more than enough wealth and treasure; more than enough pleasure — and although he delighted in the work, he was not satisfied (Ecclesiastes 2:4 – 11). In contrast, the Bible describes the Israelites during that time as being satisfied and happy, living "in safety, each man under his own vine and fig tree" (1 Kings 4:20, 25). The vine and fig tree are an image of the *gan*, the fruitful inheritance of land God gave to his people that he promised would provide "just enough" if they faithfully obeyed him.

What is your picture of the "good life"? Is it more like Solomon's, or more like the life of someone who is satisfied with God's provision of a vine or fig tree?

How does the picture you most desire relate to your relationship with God, specifically your trust in his daily provision for you?

We live in a culture that not only says we can have the "good life," but that we deserve it in great abundance. (Perhaps even Solomon might be a bit embarrassed by our craving for excess!) In light of what God taught the Israelites about depending on him and his faithful provision, what do you think he would like you to learn about what is "enough" and his faithfulness in providing for those who obey him?

How do you think God views our requests for him to provide things that far exceed what most people in the world have?

God's ongoing provision for the Israelites was clearly connected to their relationship with him — their trust and their obedience to his commands.

To what extent do you expect God to provide for you regardless of your commitment to cultivate an intimate relationship with him?

To what extent do you truly believe that you can trust God to provide what you need as you need it and that he will never forsake you?

Memorize

Keep your lives free from the love of money and be content with what you have, because God has said, "Never will I leave you; never will I forsake you."

Hebrews 13:5

Day Four | Do Not Forget

The Very Words of God

When you have eaten and are satisfied, praise the LORD your God for the good land he has given you. Be careful that you do not forget the LORD your God, failing to observe his commands, his laws and his decrees that I am giving you this day.

Deuteronomy 8:10 – 11

Bible Discovery

The Most Difficult Test

As the Israelites approached the Promised Land, Moses challenged them to obey these words: "Love the LORD your God with all your heart and with all your soul and with all your strength.... Be careful that you do not forget the LORD, who brought you out of Egypt, out of the land of slavery" (Deuteronomy 6:5, 12).

Moses was warning them against thinking that the hardest times were past. Yes, the heat of the desert, the limited diet, and the lack of water they experienced in the desert tested their faith and commitment to obey God, but a greater challenge was yet to come. Moses said, in effect, "Your toughest test was not when you were wandering in the desert wondering if you would survive. The real test of what is in your heart is when you are free, successful, have comfortable homes, and are doing well."

1. Deuteronomy records Moses' words to the Israelites as they prepared to receive God's gift of the Promised Land. Read each of the following portions as if you are part of that generation of Israelites that spent forty years in the desert experiencing an intimate relationship with God and learning to follow (obey) his every word.

   a. *Deuteronomy 8:1 - 10.* How has God proven himself faithful by leading you through the difficult situations in the desert? Are you confident of his love and provision for you? As you consider what he is now asking of you, how do you feel about your willingness to obey and your ability to fulfill his expectations? Is your heart full of praise for what he has done and is about to do?

   b. *Deuteronomy 8:11 - 18.* Moses changes his tone. What is his concern for your future? What is the risk of success that lies at the root of forgetting God and not being

thankful for his blessings? What is the only antidote for
this danger?

c. *Deuteronomy 11:10 - 15.* In what way will the land itself
bear witness to God's faithful provision? Why is the
land God has chosen the perfect setting to teach you to
"remember" and not forget that he has provided everything you need?

2. When that first generation entered the Promised Land,
they remembered God, but what happened as generations
passed? (See Isaiah 17:10 - 11; Jeremiah 2:1 - 2, 5 - 8, 13,
31 - 32.)

3. When people become "successful" and forget that their
prosperity comes from the hand of God, they often become
self-sufficient, prideful, and ungrateful. These attitudes not
only impact our relationship with God, they affect our relationships with other people and hinder our ability to display
God's character to the world.

a. What attitude and resulting actions did God command
his people to demonstrate concerning the poor and
aliens (foreigners)? (See Leviticus 19:9 - 10, 33 - 34;
23:22; Deuteronomy 15:4 - 11.)

b. When God's people became successful, blessed, and
forgot God, who else did they forget, and in what ways
is this a violation of God's purpose for his people? (See
Isaiah 3:14 – 15; 10:1 – 2; 58:6 – 8; Amos 5:1, 11 – 12;
Zechariah 7:8 – 12.)

THINK ABOUT IT

The Three Desert "Tests"

God tested his people three times on their journey to Mount Sinai. (Each test is explored in depth in *Faith Lessons vol. 9: Fire on the Mountain*, Session One, "The Lord Heals You: Marah and Elim" and Session Two, "Not by Bread Alone: Manna and Water from the Rock.") Through these tests, God demonstrated his commitment to meet the Israelites' basic needs and revealed whether they would love him with all their heart and soul. They would face the hardest test—whether or not they would love him with all their strength—in the Promised Land.

Test One: The Bitter Water at Marah

Exodus 15:22 – 27

After crossing the Red Sea, the Israelites traveled for three days without finding water. When they did find water, it was too bitter to drink so they grumbled against Moses. No doubt the harsh reality of the desert had stripped away their sense of security and forced them to realize that they could not handle the circumstances they faced. God sweetened the water and taught them to listen to his voice and do what is right in his eyes.

How have you reacted when you (or other people you know) have faced crises that you could not handle on your own, such as physical danger, natural disaster, or financial difficulties? What do you think God wanted you to learn from this experience about him and his provision? What insights does your experience provide into why the Israelites reacted the way they did at Marah?

continued on next page . . .

Test Two: Craving the Food of Egypt

Exodus 16; Deuteronomy 8:2–3, 14–16; Psalm 78:12–19; Joshua 5:12

When the Israelites became hungry, they craved the food they had enjoyed in Egypt. They spoke harshly to Moses and Aaron, accusing them of leading them into the desert to starve them to death. The Israelites had not yet learned to trust God; their dependence on Egypt's provision remained. God responded patiently, generously, and faithfully with a daily provision of bread from heaven.

We often count on our strength and abilities to provide for our basic needs, yet God wants us to look to him to provide all that we need. In what way(s) might God be trying to "mold" you through difficult circumstances in which you cannot provide for your needs so that you will learn daily dependence on him?

Test Three: No Water at Rephidim

Exodus 17:1–7; Deuteronomy 6:13–19; Psalm 95:6–9

When God led the Israelites to Rephidim, they found no water to drink. They quarreled with Moses, who rightly interpreted that their real issue was with God. They demanded that God prove his presence to them. God considered their attitude and actions to be a serious offense against him, yet he provided a stream of water for them from "his mountain," Mount Sinai (Horeb).

In what ways are we demanding or defiant toward God? Do you, for example, put God to the test when you encounter difficult circumstances? If you demand that he prove himself before you trust him, are you doubting his ability? His promises? His faithfulness?

Although it is easy for us to judge the Israelites for their response to God's testing, we need to remember that none of us ever obeys God perfectly. The real question is, did they seek God's forgiveness and learn to obey him in the future? With each test, God trained his people to trust him moment by moment and live by every word that came from his mouth. They often failed at first, but God slowly molded them into the people he wanted them to be.

Reflection

The greatest tests often do not come in the midst of crisis but in the midst of success, plenty, and comfort when we are tempted to forget what brought us success in the first place. Eventually, the Israelites did "forget" God. Books of the Bible reveal the dreadful consequences — to the Israelites, to their witness of the character of God, to the needy within their community, to the future of their nation, and even to the land God gave to them. How different it would have been if they had continued to "remember" the Lord who brought them out of slavery.

To what extent do you, people you know, and your culture in general "forget" God and take the credit that he deserves?

If you have done this, what were the consequences and what brought you back to "remembering" God and what he has done?

Could the dire scenarios Moses said would happen to the people and nation that forgets him happen to you and/or your culture? Why or why not?

To what degree are you, your faith community, and/or your culture characterized by a deep sense of dependence on God?

In what ways do you express your dependence and gratitude?

What impact does your expression of dependence have on other people and their perception of God?

God wants his people to look to him for everything they need and to live by his every word. To help you remember all that God provides for you and how he wants you to remember him and obey him, select some portions of Deuteronomy chapters 6, 8, and 11 and begin reading them every day. Take note of the ways in which your perspective changes.

The apostle Paul wrote, "Whatever you do, do it all for the glory of God" (1 Corinthians 10:31). In what ways will making this your goal in every circumstance, thought, and action help you to "remember" God?

Memorize

When the LORD your God brings you into the land he swore to your fathers, to Abraham, Isaac and Jacob, to give you — a land with large, flourishing cities you did not build, houses filled with all kinds of good things you did not provide, wells you did not dig, and vineyards and olive groves you did not plant — then when you eat and are satisfied, be careful that you do not forget the LORD, who brought you out of Egypt, out of the land of slavery.

Deuteronomy 6:10 – 12

Day Five | The Tragedy of Be'ushim

The Very Words of God

My loved one had a vineyard
on a fertile hillside.
He dug it up and cleared it of stones
and planted it with the choicest vines.
He built a watchtower in it
and cut out a winepress as well.
Then he looked for a crop of good grapes,
but it yielded only bad fruit....
What more could have been done for my vineyard
than I have done for it?
When I looked for good grapes,
why did it yield only bad?

Isaiah 5:1 – 2, 4

Bible Discovery

When God's People Produce Bad Fruit

When God's people entered Canaan (Israel), they no doubt were overjoyed by the blessings God provided. But over time, they forgot that God was the source of all blessings. When they began to take credit for what *they* had accomplished and accumulated, their attitudes changed. They lost compassion for less-fortunate people, disregarded the work and words of God, denied justice for the innocent, and pursued their own satisfaction.

Through the prophet Isaiah, God pronounced judgment using the metaphor of a vineyard, a *gan*, an image his people readily understood. Isaiah 5 portrays God as a meticulous farmer who painstakingly created and cared for a beautiful vineyard — a fertile *gan* — on a hillside. This vineyard represented God's people, and with all the work the farmer put into it, it should have produced an abundant harvest of wonderful fruit.[2] Instead, it produced *be'ushim* — a crop of stinking, rotten, worthless grapes.

DATA FILE
Building a Gan

By looking at the beautiful *ganim* on the hillsides, it's difficult to imagine the work required to build and maintain them. The Judah Mountains cover approximately forty miles from north to south and twenty miles east to west. The rock of the mountain ridges is hard Eocene limestone interspersed with layers of softer Cenomanian limestone, which erodes faster and gives the hillsides a "staircase" appearance of successive, flat, horizontal surfaces with little, if any, topsoil. Because farmland is scarce in this region, ancient people "created" farmland by terracing the hillsides.

Typically, each layer of harder limestone is four to six feet thick, between ten and forty feet wide, as much as one hundred feet in length. The front edges of these natural limestone layers were used as a foundation to build a terraced garden. Farmers built complex stone walls that formed a terrace behind which they placed thick, alternating layers of gravel and soil.

The terrace design minimized hillside erosion, allowed the porous, soil-gravel bed to absorb the maximum amount of rainwater while draining surplus water to the terrace below. If cared for each year, these terraces last for millennia. Abraham may well have known about some of the terraces being used today!

Once it is built, cultivating a *gan* requires hard, physical labor. There is no space in a *gan* for an ox- or donkey-drawn plow. In fact, the word translated "cultivate" (Isaiah 5:6) is literally "hoe" in Hebrew. This refers to the tool the farmer used to loosen hardened soil so it would absorb rainfall and to kill the ever-present weeds and thorns that would prevent a good crop. Even today, a *gan* (vineyard) requires constant attention to preserve its walls and prevent weeds from taking over.

APART FROM A FEW REMNANTS OF ANCIENT WALLS, IT'S HARD TO BELIEVE THAT THIS HILLSIDE WAS ONCE COVERED BY BEAUTIFUL *GANIM*.

continued on next page . . .

When the Romans expelled the Jews from their homeland, the foreigners who took their place were unfamiliar with agricultural practices in the land, so they neglected the *ganim*. They allowed the terrace walls to deteriorate, and the precious topsoil eroded away. In many places where there once were beautiful, fertile *ganim*, there is now nothing left that will produce fruit. Instead, the hillsides are covered by briars and thorns, just as Isaiah wrote in his song about God's vineyard (Isaiah 5:6).

1. Apart from its meaning as God's revelation, Isaiah 5:1 – 7 is a beautiful example of ancient poetry. Spend some time reading it and take in the vivid picture and passionate action it portrays. Your understanding of the vineyard image will be further enhanced by reading Psalm 80:8 – 16; Jeremiah 2:21; and John 15:1 – 4.

   a. In the metaphor of the vineyard, how hard had God worked to prepare the vineyard for his people and his people for the vineyard? List some of the specific things he did.

   b. What type of vines did God plant in the vineyard? (See Isaiah 5:2.)

DID YOU KNOW?

In Hebrew, the word translated "choice" is *soreq*, which are the very best vines. To this day, grapevines grown on the terraced hillsides of the Judah Mountains are propagated by cuttings taken during winter from the previous year's shoots. Each cutting is typically about twelve inches long and has several buds. When it is planted in fertile soil, with sufficient moisture, each cutting produces roots and becomes a new vine.

c. What did God do that showed how much he valued
    his vineyard and was committed to protecting it? (See
    Isaiah 5:2.)

DATA FILE
Watchtowers and Winepresses

In the vineyards of Israel today, you can still see ancient stone watchtowers from which families protected their grapes and olives from animal and human intruders. During busy times such as spring pruning or the fall harvest, people slept in these towers rather than making the long walk back to their homes each evening. During hot days, the towers offered welcome shade. The towers may also have provided places to store farming tools and oil, wine, and grain until they could be transported back to the farmer's home.

Nearly every terraced hillside had one or more winepresses that were cut out of limestone bedrock and plastered to prevent leakage. They were generally small, five feet by ten feet with a two- to three-foot basin on one side to catch the juice. As the grapes were tread, juice poured into a vat after passing through a small filtering chamber that collected skins, pits, and pulp.

Winepresses were located in the *ganim* to reduce the labor needed to transport the grapes and to protect them from damage during transport. During biblical times, the winepress was often a place of joy and singing as God's people celebrated his gift of fertile land and a bountiful harvest. The winepress mentioned in Isaiah 5:1–2 indicates that God expected his people to produce a rich harvest in his vineyard.

DID YOU KNOW?

What Is Be'ushim?

The English translation of Isaiah 5:4 describes the fruit the vinedresser found as "bad," "worthless," or "wild." The Hebrew word, *be'ushim*, comes from a root that implies "stinking" or "rotten" (Exodus 5:21; 7:18, 21; 16:20.) This term likely referred to stunted, rotten grapes that the farmer found in his vineyard in spite of all his efforts and expectations. Imagine God's pain in having trained his people in faith and obedience in the desert and later watching them not only forget him and his commands but turn to worship other gods!

2. After all of the effort God expended as keeper of the vineyard, he expected an abundant harvest. What did he chisel from hard limestone in anticipation of receiving a significant harvest over a long period of time? (See Isaiah 5:2.)

3. What kind of "fruit" did God expect his people to produce in the vineyard he had prepared for them? (See Exodus 19:2 – 6; 23:9; Leviticus 19:1 – 19, 33 – 37; Deuteronomy 24:10 – 14, 17 – 22; Isaiah 5:7; 43:10 – 12.)

Imagine what it would be like to live where fruit like this grew in abundance! In what ways would such a harvest be a fulfillment of God's plan for his people to join with him in restoring *shalom* to his world?

What kind of fruit did God find instead, and how did he respond? (See Isaiah 5:4 – 7.)

FOR GREATER UNDERSTANDING
God Expected Zedekah, but Heard Ze'akah

A clever wordplay used in the "Song of the Vineyard" (Isaiah 5:1 – 7) is evident in Hebrew but not in English. God went to his vineyard expecting to find the fruit of justice and righteousness — *zedekah* in Hebrew. Instead, he heard *ze'akah* — a heart-wrenching wailing uttered in response to great pain, suffering, and despair. The worst part was, his own people — the people whom he had taught to hear *ze'akah* with the same compassion with which he heard it — had caused those cries by shedding innocent blood instead of providing justice! What grief that harvest must have caused the farmer.

NOTE: To further explore the meaning of *ze'akah* and God's response to it, please reference *Faith Lessons vol. 9: Fire on the Mountain,* session three, "Their Blood Cried Out: Israel Becomes a Community."

Reflection

Although we may not be as familiar with the images of the *ganim* or vineyard as people during biblical times, God is still the keeper of the vineyard. He still cares deeply for his vineyard and has given the best of his resources, labor, and sacrifice in order to make it produce a bountiful harvest of wonderful fruit.

Who is represented in God's vineyard today, and what does God still desire his vineyard to produce? (See John 15:1 – 4.)

How does the metaphorical vineyard of Isaiah 5 (you may want to read it again) help you to understand how important God's vineyard is to him and how much effort he has expended on your behalf —

To bless you?

To prepare you to bear the full fruit of righteousness?

The Bible draws a stark contrast between a harvest of good fruit and bad fruit. Consider what the Bible says about the fruit God wants his vineyard to produce and God's response to the bad fruit he finds. Then write down examples of the fruit that is produced by your culture, your faith community, and your life.

The Fruit of God's Vineyard	The Fruit God Desires: Deut. 24:17–22	The Fruit God Discovers: Isa. 3:8–9, 13–15
The fruit of my culture		
The fruit of my faith community		
The fruit of my life		

Is the fruit of your culture, your faith community, and your life a delight to God's eyes — a reason to celebrate a good harvest — or does it grieve his heart?

What in your life needs to change in order to grow the pleasing fruit of righteousness that God desires your life to produce?

What, for example, do you choose in life that is more important than God's ongoing work of discipline and training in righteousness?

If you are a follower of Jesus, you are called to bear fruit in God's vineyard. Ask him, as the vinedresser, to provide the strength, commitment, discipline, and supporting community you need to be a beautiful *gan* that bears choice spiritual "fruit."

A WELL-WATERED GARDEN

The people of the Bible used concrete images of everyday experience to define and describe their understanding of themselves and their world. For example, they came to understand God through life's experiences — from the wind (Hebrew: *ruach* or Spirit) that blew, hearing his voice in the thunder, or recognizing his presence in fire. In their world, truth was perceived through experience more than by thought, so faith became more like a relationship they experienced than a creed they professed.

Furthermore, these ancient people typically communicated through verbal pictures rather than the abstract ideas that Western thought prefers. Nowhere is this more evident than in the biblical text. Thus the writers of the Bible describe God as their *shepherd*, who cared for his people — his *flock* — by leading them to *green pastures* and *still water*. By his *strong arm* he defeated their enemies. He was their *king* and their *father*; they were his *children*.

God used these cultural images and practices to communicate his message in ways his people would understand. When he sent Jesus the Messiah, for example, he did so as a Father who was willing to sacrifice his son — much as Abraham, their patriarch, had been willing. Jesus, God's Son, became the Lamb who died on Passover and rose from the dead as the First Fruit.

Recognizing how the Bible often conveys its message through familiar, everyday images, we should not be surprised that images of farming and shepherding frequently describe the nature of God, his people, and their relationship. After all, agriculture was the mainstay of the people of God's land, which in turn portrayed an even greater Promised Land to come! One particularly rich biblical image is that of a hillside vineyard or garden (Hebrew, *gan*; plural, *ganim*), which we explored a bit in the previous session.

In this session, we will further explore the significance of the images of the fruitful vineyard or *gan*. These terraced gardens are carefully tended to this day and, just as when his people first entered the Promised Land, God still calls his people to be like a fruitful vineyard. He still promises that they will be like a "well-watered garden" if they obey his commands.

In order to bear fruit, each *gan* requires ongoing care — not just from one farmer, but from everyone who farmed *ganim* on a particular hillside. It took extensive, cooperative labor to create the terraces, dig cisterns and irrigation channels, build and repair walls, bring in and cultivate topsoil, plant and harvest crops, and effectively utilize rainfall and springs. In order for each family to have "a well-watered" garden, cooperation was essential. The *ganim* were (and are) successful only if the community works together. Without cooperation, for example, cascading water during the rainy season could break through the walls of one *gan* and destroy others below it. As we'll see, the cooperative, community nature of producing a fruitful vineyard has significant implications for the community of God's people today.

Opening Thoughts (3 minutes)

The Very Words of God

> If you do away with the yoke of oppression, with the pointing finger and malicious talk, and if you spend yourselves in behalf of the hungry and satisfy the needs of the oppressed, then your light will rise in the darkness, and your night will become like the noonday.
> The LORD will guide you always; he will satisfy your needs in a sun-scorched land and will strengthen your frame. You will be like a well-watered garden, like a spring whose waters never fail.

Isaiah 58:9 – 11

Think About It

When we think of what sin brings into our world, a variety of mental images come to mind. We have seen — to one degree or another — what chaos looks like. We can describe it in vivid detail.

In contrast, which words, phrases, or images would you use to describe what the community of God's people brings into the world when it is at its very best, bearing the fruit of righteousness in abundance?

DVD Notes (23 minutes)

The three crops of a fertile *gan*—figs, olives, grapes

The hard work of tending a *gan*—the crop, the soil, the walls

The community of God's people has a mission in the vineyard

Have you nurtured the soil and repaired the walls?

Have you trained other people to carry on the work?

DVD Discussion (7 minutes)

1. Using the map on page 247, locate the cities of Jerusalem, Hebron, and Beersheba in the Judah Mountains. The *ganim* where this video was filmed are just west of Jerusalem, part of an area about forty miles long and twenty miles wide where this type of farming was practiced. To the west are the foothills between the coastal plain and the mountains. To the east is rugged desert wilderness that drops steeply toward the Dead Sea.

2. What did you feel and think when you saw the fertile, terraced *gan* close up? When you saw the ancient stone walls, and the "baby" olives and grapes?

3. In what ways did the close, compact nature of the *ganim* give you a new picture of what God intends his community of people to be?

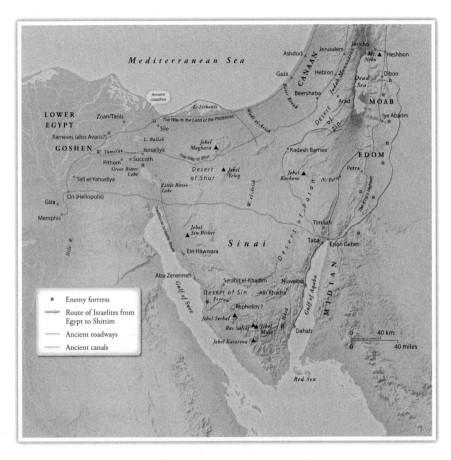

What kind of close connection and cooperation between individual families can you now envision taking place in the *ganim*?

What is at risk for the whole *ganim* if even one farmer fails to carefully maintain the walls of his *gan*? If he lets it get overgrown with weeds or briars?

What do you think is the significance of the picture of community in the *ganim* — that everyone rises or falls together — to your faith community?

4. What is your response to the challenge to be a community and take action to not only care for and preserve the *ganim* but to leave a heritage of fertile "soil" that will enable those who follow to be fruitful for God?

Which specific things — little things, big things — can we as individuals and as a faith community do to not only pray for a good harvest but to create the fertile "soil" in which faith in God can grow and, with his blessing, provide abundant harvests for many years?

Small Group Bible Discovery and Discussion (20 minutes)

The Blessings of a Well-Watered Garden

Throughout the Bible, from the Garden of Eden to eternity, God's world is often portrayed through metaphors of a garden, and God's people are often envisioned as a fertile *gan*. The lessons conveyed by this imagery are as relevant for us today as they were for people who lived during ancient times. So let's explore some characteristics of a garden — particularly a well-watered garden — to see how God provides for it and what he expects it to produce.

1. What beautiful metaphor describes the Israelites — the people of God — and what does it reveal about the life God wants his people to enjoy? (See Isaiah 58:11; Jeremiah 31:11 – 14.)

   What is the source of the goodness and abundance described in these passages?

   Is the blessing portrayed something to be received and enjoyed by a few people, or to be experienced by the entire community?

   In what ways would the picture of God's people being like well-watered *ganim* demonstrate his presence in the world?

2. No garden can thrive or provide the rich blessings of a fruitful harvest without water, so knowing the water source and how to access it is essential.

   a. What is the ideal picture of a well-watered garden, and what does this indicate about the source of its fruitfulness? (See Genesis 13:10.)

    b.   According to Jeremiah 2:13; 17:13 and Isaiah 58:11, who is the "spring" of living water whose blessings make a garden well watered?

    c.   What waters God's city, and whose blessing does that water represent? (See Psalm 46:1 – 5.)

3.   What determines whether or not a garden will be blessed with water and a fruitful harvest? (See Deuteronomy 11:8 – 17; Jeremiah 5:23 – 25.)

How would you describe the nature of God's involvement with his people and the land he gave to them?

What impact does the kind of relationship God's people choose to have with him have on the fruitfulness of the garden?

4.   Consider how these garden images, particularly those that describe the blessing, joy, and abundance of a well-watered garden, add to your understanding of the "fruit" God expects his people to produce. What impact would you expect the

"fruit" described in Isaiah 58:6-10 to have in our communities if those of us who follow Jesus the Messiah were producing abundant fruit today?

DATA FILE
A Well-Watered Gan—A Cooperative Endeavor

Nearly all of the approximately twenty-five to thirty inches of rain the Judah Mountains receive falls during November through April. So ancient farmers built terraced hillside gardens (*gan*; plural, *ganim*) not only to provide flat places on which to cultivate crops but to help distribute rainfall so the land would be productive. The design of the terrace walls and layers of soil and gravel placed behind them allowed each *gan* to absorb as much water as possible. Remaining moisture then drained slowly through the soil and gravel layers to the terrace below, and so on until excess water drained into the valley below. Without protection by man-made walls, the sparsely distributed topsoil could not absorb such heavy rainfall and would be washed away.

continued on next page . . .

So a hillside of well-watered gardens (Isaiah 58:11; Jeremiah 31:12) required a cooperative effort. It depended first on God's blessing of rain (Deuteronomy 11:11–12), which was conditional on whether or not God's people faithfully obeyed his commands. Second, the entire hillside had to be farmed as a unit through the cooperation of the entire community.

A village would choose an appropriate hillside and together organize and plan how the terraced gardens would be laid out. After completing their *ganim*, each family would care for its respective *gan* —and the *ganim* of others, knowing that the hillside could only be successfully cultivated if *every* terrace functioned as it was intended.

Cooperation was also required in the capture and use of water for the *ganim*. God certainly had fulfilled his promise to bring his people to a land of flowing springs (Deuteronomy 8:7). Nearly two hundred springs, most of which were used to irrigate terraced gardens, have been identified in the Judah, Bethlehem, and Hebron Mountains.[1] Ancient people often built *ganim* on particular hillsides because of the nearby springs. Farmers then cooperated to build the network of basins and channels needed to irrigate gardens at the same level or below the level of the spring. Sometimes farmers cut cisterns into the bedrock or built reservoirs to store extra water, which required them to work together in order to benefit the maximum number of people. God's gift of the land demanded his blessing and required his people to function as a caring community.

Faith Lesson (6 minutes)

Before viewing the video for this session, you may have thought that well-watered gardens were a product of individual effort: "I care for my garden (my space); you care for yours." Although that type of thinking permeates Western culture today, entire communities cooperated together in order to farm hillsides in the Judah Mountains during ancient times. Only as a community could they expect to maintain and preserve their gardens and receive the blessing of fruitful harvests.

1. As a representation of his presence in the world, God expects his *ganim*, his people, to be productive and make an impact. If you have a relationship with God through Jesus (and metaphorically are his *gan*), what fruit are you producing for the "gardener"? List specific examples.

    What things in your life — actions, thoughts, attitudes — might be preventing you from experiencing the fullness of God's living water and being a more fruitful "garden"?

    Does your work in the *ganim*, the larger community of God's people, contribute to the fruitfulness of the entire community, or are you a bit of a "lone ranger" who does whatever seems best to you? What specific things do you presently do, and what more could you do to be a more involved member of God's *ganim*?

2. Using metaphors of your time and your world, how would you describe the fruit God wants his *ganim* to produce? (To help you get started, list specific examples of what Isaiah 58:9 – 10 would look like in your world.)

    How much need do you see in your world for the blessing of the rich, abundant fruit of God's well-watered garden?

    How would an abundance of that fruit demonstrate God's character and presence to the world and change the character and feel of your local community?

3. What would it be like to see a broken and hurting community transformed by God's *ganim* into a community of joy, gladness, dancing, and singing?

    How badly do you want to contribute to and be part of such a community?

What are you willing to sacrifice and how hard are you willing to work *in cooperation with* other members of your faith community to see that happen?

Closing (1 minute)

Read James 3:17 – 18 aloud together: "But the wisdom that comes from heaven is first of all pure; then peace-loving, considerate, submissive, full of mercy and good fruit, impartial and sincere. Peacemakers who sow in peace raise a harvest of righteousness."

Then pray, thanking God for his desire and commitment to restore *shalom* to his broken world. Tell him that you want to be suitable and fruitful partners in bringing his blessings and healing to your world.

Memorize

But the wisdom that comes from heaven is first of all pure; then peace-loving, considerate, submissive, full of mercy and good fruit, impartial and sincere. Peacemakers who sow in peace raise a harvest of righteousness.

James 3:17 – 18

Learning to Live by the Word and Heart of God

In-Depth Personal Study Sessions

Day One | The Olive Tree

The Very Words of God

> *I am like an olive tree flourishing in the house of God; I trust in God's unfailing love for ever and ever.*
>
> *I will praise you forever for what you have done; in your name I will hope, for your name is good. I will praise you in the presence of your saints.*
>
> **Psalm 52:8–9**

Bible Discovery

The Olive Tree: A Metaphor for God's Work in the World

The olive tree was essential to life in the ancient world, so it's not surprising that it is a significant biblical metaphor. People used olive oil for lighting, medicine, cosmetics, cooking, anointing, and as a cash crop. Olive wood, which is extremely hard and has a beautiful grain, was used in furniture building and other construction projects. Olive oil is among the foods God said would be in the Promised Land (Deuteronomy 8:7–8), and farmers cultivated olive trees in terraced hillside *ganim*. Since the biblical writers used the image of a "well-watered" garden to portray God's blessings and his relationship with his people, it is not surprising that they also used the plants of a *gan*, including the olive tree, to illustrate God's truth.

1. The olive tree is one of the common representations of God's people. The following uses of that symbolism illustrate God's relationship with his people.

a.   David compared God's people to an olive tree. What is
     the significance of where the tree was located and why it
     was flourishing? (See Psalm 52:8 – 9.)

     Would you expect an olive tree to flourish there? Why or
     why not?

     Is the picture of strength, trust, and hope something you
     long for in your life? If so, how would you find it? If not,
     why not?

b.   What happens when God's people turn away from righ-
     teousness? (See Jeremiah 11:15 – 16.)

c. What does the fruit of the olive tree tell the farmer
    about the tree, and how does he respond? (See Matthew
    3:7 – 10; 7:18 – 19.)

d. Hosea portrays what God will do for his people after
    they repent of their wayward ways. What picture does
    Hosea 14:4 – 7 present of God's faithfulness in loving and
    caring for his people and their role in displaying God's
    goodness to other people?

DATA FILE
The Life of the Olive Tree

Olive trees begin producing fruit between six and ten years of age and reach
their peak about thirty-five or more years later. Once established, these trees
may produce olives for hundreds of years, yielding a harvest of thirty or more
gallons of oil annually.

When its branches finally stop producing fruit, the tree still has a useful life.
The farmer will cut off the branches, leaving a stump several feet tall. The
tree may appear to be dead, but the following year new shoots will grow out
of the stump and become fruit-bearing branches. Or, new shoots or branches
may be grafted onto the old stump to receive nourishment from its root sys-
tem. From this new growth, the tree will once again produce many olives.

Because olive trees endure, Israel is often thought of as being God's olive
tree or grove. The gnarled stumps of olive trees thrive in rocky soil with a
minimum of rainfall. Even when their enemies cut down God's people, or
God cuts them off for bearing bad fruit (as he did when they worshiped Baal,
Jeremiah 11:17), God restores those who repent, and they soon have the
opportunity to bear fruit again.

2. The prophets used the general knowledge that new, life-giving, fruit-producing branches would sprout from the stump of a seemingly dead olive tree. Who did they say was the new shoot, or branch, that would come from the stump of Jesse (David), and how did they describe the character of this branch and the fruit it would produce? (See Isaiah 11:1 – 2; 53:2 – 6; Jeremiah 23:5; 33:15; Zechariah 3:8; 6:12.)

FOR GREATER UNDERSTANDING
Jesus from Nazareth

Sometimes people referred to Jesus, who came from Nazareth, as a Nazarene (Mark 14:67; 16:6). Although no biblical prophet says, "He will be called a Nazarene," Jesus' identity as a Nazarene fulfilled ancient prophecies. The Greek word translated *Nazareth* (or *Nazarene*) is likely derived from the Hebrew word *netzer* that means "shoot" or "branch" and often refers to the royal line of David. The description "Jesus the Nazarene," meaning "Jesus the Branch (or shoot)," linked him to prophecies stating that the Messiah would be the "branch" that would grow out of Jesse's "stump" in the "olive grove" that was Israel.

Early Christians were known as "the Nazarene sect" (Acts 24:5). So Jesus' followers today are like shoots of an olive tree — either natural branches (Jewish) or grafted wild olive branches (Gentiles), and all of God's people are symbolized by the olive tree or olive grove. It is important for us to realize that when God broke down the wall separating Jew and Gentile, he did not invite Jews to become Gentiles; he invited Gentiles to join his people, the Jews. The olive tree is a constant reminder that Jesus is our Branch. He grew from Jewish roots, and so do we.

3. Sometimes followers of Jesus who are not Jewish act as if God gave up on his Jewish olive trees and replaced them with new ones. Romans 11:1 – 5, 11 – 24 presents a different understanding.

    a. Did God ever completely cut off (as in destroy) the "stump" of his people because of their sin? How do we know this?

    b. Who is the stump of God's olive tree today, and who are its branches?

DID YOU KNOW?

Just as shoots growing around the base of an ancient olive tree can be transplanted and become new trees, so children in a family are the "shoots" that will become the fruit-producing trees of the next generation (Psalm 128:3). These new "trees" will be of the same nature as the root stock/stump from which they came, a truth that emphasizes the importance of a family remaining faithful to the Lord. The children of today will bear fruit of the same nature as the families in which they grew up.

---

4. Olive oil had many uses in daily life. In addition to its use as a food, olive oil was used for skin care, to fuel lamps, and was taken as medicine. It also had other symbolic and spiritual uses.

    a. How was it used in relationship to the priests and their service to God? (See Exodus 29:1 – 7; Leviticus 8:12, 30.)

b. How was it used to designate certain of God's people for special roles or tasks among the people (such as kings and prophets), and what did it signify? (See 1 Samuel 10:1; 16:10 – 13; Psalm 45:7; Isaiah 61:1 – 3; Hebrews 1:9.)

c. What was Jesus anointed to do, and how did his anointing equip him to do it? (See Isaiah 61:1; Luke 4:18 – 19; Acts 10:37 – 38.)

d. Who were (and are) Jesus' anointed ones and what did (does) that anointing signify and provide? (See 2 Corinthians 1:21 – 22; 1 John 2:20, 27.)

e. How else was olive oil used by people of faith? (See James 5:14.)

5. In what way was the light of an olive oil lamp a representation of God and his people? (See Matthew 5:14; John 8:12; 1 John 1:5.)

FOR GREATER UNDERSTANDING
Olive Oil for Anointing

Olives were one of the three blessings of the Promised Land listed in Deuteronomy 6:11. Scripture links olive oil to divine blessing and the coming of God's Spirit. Oil also symbolized honor, joy, favor, and love. When used to anoint people for special tasks and appointments, olive oil symbolized God equipping that person with authority and calling that person to a specific responsibility.

Kings were anointed, as were priests, holy things, and places where God had acted. As God placed his Spirit on the person called to serve him, the oil used for outward anointing increasingly came to symbolize the Spirit that accompanied that anointing. By New Testament times, anointing had come to be viewed primarily as the inner work of the Spirit, such as on Jesus and his followers.

The Hebrew word for "anointed" is *mashiach*, from which we get our English word *Messiah*. A *mashiach* was a chosen instrument whom God anointed with his Spirit for a special task that would greatly benefit other people. Although many people were anointed during Old Testament times and every follower of Jesus is anointed by God's Spirit today, there is only one Messiah: Jesus, God's anointed. The title given to Jesus — *Christ* (from the Greek) and *Messiah* (from the Hebrew) — means "anointed" and occurs more than 375 times in the New Testament. This is yet another example of the olive-tree metaphor, in this case representing Jesus the Messiah, God's anointed priest and king.

DID YOU KNOW?

During Old Testament times, people made olive oil by pounding ripe olives to a pulp in pestles and pressing them with their feet. They then collected the pulp in reed baskets from which additional oil drained off. (Black, ripe olives often contained more than 50 percent of their weight in oil!) During Jesus' time, a large, wheel-shaped millstone was rolled in a circle to grind the olives to pulp. After the first oil was drained off, remaining pulp was placed into wicker baskets that were stacked in or over stone pits. A heavy stone weight called an olive press then pressed down on these baskets to extract remaining oil.

In Hebrew, the olive press is called a *Gath Shemanim*, from which our word "Gethsemane" is derived. So the garden where Jesus spent his last evening with his disciples was likely an olive grove, a *gan*, that had its own olive press. There, Jesus was "pressed" and sweat drops of blood while preparing to take on himself the weight of the sins of the world. To learn more about olives and the olive press, see *Faith Lessons vol. 7: Walk as Jesus Walked*, session four, "Why Christians Suffer — The Weight of Gethsemane" and *Faith Lessons vol. 4: Death and Resurrection of the Messiah*, session seven, "The Weight of the World."

Reflection

The biblical image of God's people (Israel) being represented by the olive tree adds greatly to our understanding of God's Word, the kind of relationship he desires to have with us, and the impact he wants our lives to have on other people. Jesus the Messiah is a "branch" out of one of God's (Jesse's) olive trees, and every follower of Jesus is part of his olive tree as either a natural branch or a grafted shoot. Our purpose is to produce an abundant harvest that honors God and displays his character to the world.

In light of what you have explored during this session, would you describe yourself as "God's olive tree" planted in the "house of God"? Why or why not?

What nourishment are you receiving from Jesus to produce good fruit?

To what extent do you depend on him for the nourishment to produce fruit, as opposed to trying to produce fruit on your own?

Reread Matthew 7:17 – 20 and think about what Jesus would say to you about the fruit you are producing and how you are doing it.

What has Jesus said will happen to shoots that do not produce good fruit?

What kind of fruit do you want to produce?

What kind of blessing (light) do you want to bring into your world?

What change(s) might you need to make in order to bear that kind of fruit?

Memorize

I will be like the dew to Israel; he will blossom like a lily. Like a cedar of Lebanon he will send down his roots; his young shoots will grow. His splendor will be like an olive tree.

Hosea 14:5 – 6

Day Two | The Vine

The Very Words of God

> *I am the true vine, and my Father is the gardener. He cuts off every branch in me that bears no fruit, while every branch that does bear fruit he prunes so that it will be even more fruitful. You are already clean because of the word I have spoken to you. Remain in me, and I will remain in you. No branch can bear fruit by itself; it must remain in the vine. Neither can you bear fruit unless you remain in me.*
>
> *John 15:1 – 4*

Bible Discovery

The Vine: Fruitful or Worthless?

Few cultivated crops are as dependent on the skilled work of the farmer and the proper rhythm of the seasons and rainfall as the vine. Because God's people experienced the hard labor of creating and caring for vineyards, the vine (like the well-watered garden, the olive, and the fig), was an excellent metaphor to describe the relationship between God and his people. The nature of the vine — the fact that its only value is in the fruit it bears — also helps to emphasize how important it is for God's people to "remain" in the vine so that they will bear fruit.

1. To refresh your overall picture of God's vineyard and its fruitfulness (or lack thereof) in relationship to God, read Psalm 80:7 – 19.

a. Who is symbolized as God's vine, and how deeply did God, as the farmer of the *gan*, express care for his vine? (See Psalm 80:8 – 10; Isaiah 5:7; 27:2 – 3; Jeremiah 2:4, 7, 21.)

b. What had God's beloved vine done to become unfruitful? (See Jeremiah 2:4 – 7, 21; Hosea 10:1 – 3; Amos 5:7, 10 – 13.)

c. What did God do, or allow others to do, as a consequence? (See Psalm 80:12 – 13; Isaiah 5:5 – 6; 16:8 – 10; 32:9 – 14; Amos 5:11.)

d. If the vine that had ceased producing fruit returned to him in repentance and obedience, what promise of restoration did God make? (See Jeremiah 31:2 – 5, 12 – 13; Hosea 14:1 – 7.)

e. In what ways have these images contributed to your understanding of the importance of God's vine and its fruitfulness?

FOR GREATER UNDERSTANDING
An Image of the Fruitful Vine

Ancient sources reveal that a golden vine with clusters of golden grapes as

large as a man hung in front of the temple in Jerusalem. This model of the marble temple during Jesus' time shows the vine as a decorative element on the frieze along the top of the temple. The vine represented the people of God and was placed by the temple because the "farmer" — God himself — lived within the temple.

According to tradition, Jews who came to Jerusalem for Passover went to the temple courts to sing the final psalm of the seder meal. If so, it is possible that Jesus was in the temple courts when he called himself the "true vine" (John 15:1). Regardless of where he was when he gave that teaching, the beautiful golden vine on the temple illustrates the point he made about himself.

2. God loved his people — his choice vines — so much that he expended great effort to plant and cultivate them. He expected them to produce quality fruit in abundance. It is no different today. He dearly loves his people and will do his part to make us fruitful, but we must choose to place our faith in him, love (obey) him, and allow him to work through us to bear fruit. Jesus' teaching about himself and the vineyard in John 15 will help us understand what is required to be more fruitful in our world.[2]

a. Who is the gardener, who is the true vine? (v. 1)

NOTE: The identity of the vine has changed. No matter
how much effort the farmer put into it, the human vine
of Isaiah 5:2 never bore the abundant fruit God desired.

b. What does the farmer do to branches that *don't* bear
fruit, and to branches that *do* bear fruit? (v. 2)

NOTE: The Greek word translated "cut off," *airo*, can also
mean "pick up" or "lift up." Farmers often use a forked
stick or flat stone to prop up vines that trail on the
ground. This prevents the grape clusters from touching
the soil and contracting a grape-rotting fungus. Like a
farmer, God patiently disciplines his people, lifting them
up out of the dirt that could corrupt the fruit so that they
will bear a full harvest. The farmer also prunes back
the vines when the plant is dormant in order to limit
the number of clusters the plant has to support, which
improves the quality of the next harvest.

c. What is absolutely necessary for the vines to carry out
God's mission of producing abundant, delicious fruit?
(vv. 4 – 7)

NOTE: First Corinthians 1:30 says that Jesus is our "righteousness, holiness and redemption," all of which are
necessary for producing the fruit God desires.

    d.   What specific fruit did Jesus command those who are "in" him to produce? (vv. 8 – 17) How much is this fruit like the fruit God desired from his vineyard in Isaiah 5:1 – 7?

FOR GREATER UNDERSTANDING
Parables of Two Vineyards

Like other first-century rabbis, Jesus often used parables to illustrate his teaching. His audience would have expected his parables to be based on, illustrate, or interpret stories and ideas in their Bible, so they would have understood Jesus' allusion to Isaiah's writing. With this in mind, compare the Parable of the Tenants to Isaiah's Song of the Vineyard.

Isaiah's "Song of the Vineyard" (Isa. 5:1 – 7)	Jesus' Parable of the Tenants (Matt. 21:33 – 41)
God is owner (farmer)	God is owner (farmer)
Vineyard setting	Vineyard setting
Crop is planted	Crop is planted
Implies wall was built (v. 5)	Wall was built
Dug a winepress	Dug a winepress
Built a permanent watchtower	Built a permanent watchtower
Vineyard owner sought to receive fruit, but it was bad	Vineyard was fruitful, but corrupt tenants (leaders of God's people) were unwilling to share it with the owner
Israel/God's kingdom (vineyard) failed to produce good fruit	Israel/God's kingdom (vineyard) failed to share its fruit and abused/killed those sent to gather the harvest
Owner's judgment fell on the vineyard	Owner's judgment would fall on corrupt tenants

DID YOU KNOW?
Corrupt Leadership

Jewish history and the New Testament document corruption among the priestly leaders during Jesus' time. The family of Annas (Luke 3:2; John 18:12–24; Acts 4:1–6) was in power and controlled animal trade and money changing in the temple. They charged outrageous prices, practiced extortion, and embezzled money belonging to the temple.[3]

Such corruption caused great suffering among ordinary people, particularly those who tried to follow God's directives regarding temple worship. The tenants in Jesus' parable no doubt portrayed corrupt religious leaders who were in charge of God's vineyard. They refused to heed the prophets God had sent (including Isaiah, who gave them the Song of the Vineyard!) and killed the vineyard owner's son — just as the religious leaders arranged Jesus' crucifixion and continued to persecute his followers.

Reflection

God wants us to remember our need to be totally dependent on him and to trust him to "prune us" so we can produce good fruit. We can truly do nothing of eternal significance without a personal and ongoing relationship with Jesus the Messiah that expresses itself through obedience to God. If we choose to live apart from God in disobedience, we will receive his judgment. Yet God's love for his people never fails. He will forgive when we come back to him, and will do everything possible to make us fruitful.

In what ways has your study of God's love, careful cultivation of his vineyard, and his hope for a rich harvest helped you to understand:

His insistence on complete obedience to his Word?

His determination to cut out or prune everything that would diminish the harvest?

As Westerners, we like to approach life as independent, self-determined individuals. How willing are you to "be in" Jesus and trust God, as the vinedresser, to prune away everything that will hinder your fruitfulness and to nourish you with everything you need to produce a rich harvest?

What part of that process do you most fear or resist?

What disobedience might be preventing you from producing the spiritual fruit that God looks forward to seeing in your life?

How willing are you to confess your sin, ask for his forgiveness, and choose to follow (obey) him in every area of life?

Just as God "prunes" his vines for the sake of a better harvest, those of us who follow Jesus sometimes need to "cut back" on things we do. So set aside some time to evaluate your life and consider, for example, if:

Your career is hurting your fruitfulness in your community?

Your heavy involvement in your faith community is limiting your fruitfulness in relationship to your family?

Your life is so out of balance that your health is suffering and you are too weak to produce good, abundant fruit?

Sometimes God allows us to experience pain and stress in order to show us that we need pruning! What is he showing you?

Memorize

You did not choose me, but I chose you and appointed you to go and bear fruit — fruit that will last. Then the Father will give you whatever you ask in my name. This is my command: Love each other.

John 15:16 – 17

Day Three | The Fig Tree

The Very Words of God

When I found Israel, it was like finding grapes in the desert; when I saw your fathers, it was like seeing the early fruit on the fig tree.

Hosea 9:10

Bible Discovery

The Fig Tree: A Picture of Shalom

The fig tree was among the most favored trees in the world of the Bible. Fig trees grew in the Garden of Eden and can still be found in the terraced farms (*ganim*) of the Judah Mountains. The mature tree produces succulent, sweet fruit that ripens gradually and can be picked during a period of several months. Its broad, spreading branches and large leaves provide cooling shade. The ability to sit under one's own fig tree and vines symbolized the hope of God's people for the restoration of God's *shalom*.

1. During Old Testament times, what images of peace, security, and God's blessing did the fig tree represent? (See 1 Kings 4:25; 2 Kings 20:7; Joel 2:21 – 22; Micah 4:4; Zechariah 3:10.)

   In what ways do these images add to your understanding of God's *shalom*?

2. To what did God compare his people, and what does this reveal about the depth of God's love for them? (See Jeremiah 24:2 – 7; Hosea 9:10.)

DATA FILE
Figs and the Fig Tree[4]

- One of the species with which God blessed the Promised Land (Deuteronomy 8:7 – 8).
- Still commonly found in terraced farms (*ganim*) in the Judah Mountains.
- Generally becomes fruitful after seven years; has been known to bear fruit for fifty years.
- At maturity has large, widely spread branches with large leaves that provide significant shade.
- Sheds its leaves during winter; young figs start growing before new leaves develop.
- Produces ripening fruit, which gives a pleasant smell, for nearly half the year.

continued on next page . . .

**A MATURE FIG TREE PROVIDES A LARGE AREA OF DENSE
SHADE — A WELCOME RELIEF FROM THE SCORCHING
SUN OF THE MIDDLE EAST.**

- Figs are the only fruit to ripen during the hot, Middle Eastern summer and, therefore, are highly prized (Jeremiah 40:10–12).
- The first ripe figs, reportedly the sweetest (Isaiah 28:4; Nahum 3:12), are awaited eagerly and may have been the closest thing to candy that God's people enjoyed. Late-ripening figs are not as sweet and desirable (Jeremiah 24:1–10; Micah 7:1).
- Sun-dried figs were pressed into cakes that did not spoil easily and provided excellent energy — the first "power bar" (1 Samuel 25:18; 2 Samuel 16:1–2; 1 Chronicles 12:40).
- Figs were used as a curative or poultice (2 Kings 20:7).

3. The beautiful images of *shalom* portrayed by the fig tree also led to the use of the tree as a warning and symbol of God's coming judgment if his people did not remain faithful to him. What did the fig tree symbolize in the following passages?

Text	The Fate of the Fig Tree If God's People Are Unfaithful
Isa. 9:8–10	
Jer. 5:17; 8:13	
Hos. 2:12–13	
Joel 1:6–7, 12, 15	
Amos 4:9	

4. Fig trees were prominent in vineyards and gardens during Jesus' day, so the image of a fruitful fig tree was still meaningful to people and Jesus used it in his teaching. Luke 13:1 – 9 records a parable Jesus told about a fig tree in a garden.

   a. Who does the fig tree represent, and what does this parable reveal about the caretaker and his love for the fig tree?

   b. In light of the discussion that preceded Jesus' telling of the parable, what do you think he wanted his audience to realize about God, their fruitfulness, their need for repentance, and their inclination to judge others?

   c. How patient is God in giving every person who knows him time to bear good fruit, time to correct their sinful ways and walk with him?

THINK ABOUT IT

God desires all people to know and believe in Jesus as their Messiah. In its cultural context, the Luke 13 parable relates to anyone — to any "fig tree" — who has heard Jesus' message but has chosen not to repent or who feels morally superior to others who suffer. God works patiently to give people time to bear fruit — the fruit of repentance and a righteous walk with him. Eventually God's patience runs out, however. Both John the Baptist (Luke 3:9) and Jesus (Luke 13:6 – 8) warned of God's inevitable judgment if people who hear do not repent: the tree will be cut down.

5. The fig tree, as a symbol of God's people, specifically represents the leaders (Proverbs 27:18), and most of the opposition Jesus faced came from the Jewish leadership. In light of what you have learned about fig trees, take a fresh look at Matthew 21:1 – 11, 18 – 20 and Mark 11:12 – 26.

    a. Since figs appear on the tree before the leaves, what should a person have expected to find on an apparently healthy fig tree such as this one? What did Jesus find instead?

    b. What does the "gardener" do with fig trees that don't produce fruit? (See Luke 3:9; 13:6 – 8.)

    c. When Jesus cursed the tree, what happened to it, and how is this immediate result like what the gardener would have done to it?

    d.   Rabbis often used physical representations of the subject of their teaching to make a point. Given the fact that this incident took place in the midst of several confrontations Jesus had with the Jewish leaders, what message do you think his action against the fig tree conveyed?

FOR GREATER UNDERSTANDING

"I Saw You ... Under the Fig Tree"

The fig tree was a symbol of God's people, specifically those who are masters or leaders. Proverbs 27:18 reads: "He who tends a fig tree will eat its fruit, and he who looks after his master will be honored." Although a fruitful fig tree demands much care and effort, the reward of its sweet fruit is worth the effort. In a similar way, "looking after" one's master leads to the reward of honor. The meaning of this imagery helps us to understand what took place when Jesus called Nathaniel to be his disciple (John 1:43–51).

During Jesus' day disciples called their teacher (rabbi) "master" or "lord." Disciples left everything to travel with their rabbi so that they could observe his every action, hear his every word, and become like him. A disciple would obtain and prepare the rabbi's food, carry his pack, provide protection in the countryside, row the boat, and provide any other help he might need. In return, the disciple received the rabbi's instruction and example—priceless in comparison. So a good teacher, a rabbi, is like a fig tree. Tending or serving him requires much effort, but like ripe fruit the result is a delicacy worth every effort.

The phrase "tend a fig tree" (Proverbs 27:18) became synonymous with studying or serving (Hebrew, *shimmush*) one's master or rabbi. "Sitting under a fig tree" meant studying with a teacher. So some scholars interpret Jesus as telling Nathaniel, "I know you are an exceptional student, having spent many hours studying or listening to a rabbi." Nathaniel must have been overjoyed at the possibility of "sitting under a fig tree" with rabbi Jesus.

Reflection

God's overall message to his people through the fig tree metaphor is clear: be faithful and fruitful, or be cut off. God, the "gardener," expects his fig trees to bear succulent fruit, and he will judge everyone who hears the truth about Jesus but refuses to repent or to produce the fruit of righteousness (obedience to God).

Think about the images of God's *shalom* that a fruitful fig tree brought to people in biblical times — sweet, candy-like fruit and refreshing shade on a hot day. How would you describe the *shalom* that God might want to bring to your world through *your* fruitful life?

What is your desire and commitment to figuratively "sit under a fig tree" with Jesus and seek to observe, learn from, and ultimately become like him?

If you are doing this, what fruit is that experience producing in your life? If you are not doing this, what is hindering you?

In what ways are you "serving" your rabbi like a farmer tends his fig tree, and what fruit is that experience producing in your life?

If God is the "caretaker," and you are the "fig tree," what might be his assessment of your fruitfulness right now?

Would he have the ax ready to chop at the root, or would he patiently give you time to bear spiritual fruit — including the fruit of repentance?

Which thing(s) in your life may be hindering your fruitfulness, and are you willing to ask for God's forgiveness and turn away from them so that you will become more fruitful?

Day Four | God's Community: Tending the Soil of a Fertile Hillside

The Very Words of God

> *Jacob said to Joseph, "God Almighty appeared to me at Luz in the land of Canaan, and there he blessed me and said to me, 'I am going to make you fruitful and will increase your numbers. I will make you a community of peoples, and I will give this land as an everlasting possession to your descendants after you.'"*
>
> **Genesis 48:3 – 4**

Bible Discovery

Ganim that Endure: Preparing and Preserving the Soil for the Next Generation

When the Israelites arrived in the Promised Land, God gave each family in each tribe a small plot of land as an eternal inheritance. The Israelites were to care for their inheritance as the part of God's world for which they were responsible. They were not to sell their land, nor were they to take land from anyone else.[5] It was both a family and community responsibility to preserve for future generations the land God had provided. In many areas of Israel, that family inheritance was a *gan*. Although a *gan* usually had only three or four olive trees, a fig tree, and a few vines, it could sustain a family for generations. But it took commitment and hard work to maintain a fertile, well-watered *gan* that would keep producing an abundant harvest.

1. What responsibility did God give to Adam in the Garden of Eden? (See Genesis 2:15.)

    How was this like the Israelites' responsibility to prepare and preserve the soil of their inheritance, the soil of their *gan*?

2. Who alone is responsible (and able) to make trees and vines grow and produce fruit? (See Deuteronomy 11:11 – 14; Isaiah 55:10 – 11.)

LOOKING DOWN ON A *GAN* FROM ABOVE PROVIDES THE BEST VIEW OF THE FERTILE, ROCKY SOIL THAT IS ESSENTIAL TO THE SUCCESSFUL CULTIVATION OF STEEP HILLSIDES. THE WALLS HOLD THE SOIL AT EXACTLY THE RIGHT DEPTH TO HOLD THE RAINWATER NEEDED FOR THE OLIVES AND GRAPES.

Why then is it so important for God's people to tend the soil?

How much difference does the soil really make at harvest time? (See Mark 4:1 – 8.)

THINK ABOUT IT

The ancient Israelites expended great effort in building terraces on steep hill-sides to keep precious topsoil from washing way. They worked hard to place layers of gravel and soil behind the walls to soak up the maximum amount of rainwater and provide an environment in which crops such as olives, figs, and grapes could be cultivated and thrive. They knew that:

- *if* their terrace walls did not hold the soil at exactly the right depth to retain the necessary amount of rainwater
- *if* weeds and briars were allowed to grow in the soil and deprive the good plants of water
- *if* a wall collapsed and the topsoil washed away
- *if* the soil became depleted of nutrients

their gardens would be less fruitful. No wonder the hillside farmers needed to think and act as a cooperative community!

3. The mission of God's people is to be like a fertile "well-watered garden" on a hillside (Isaiah 58:11) where our "soil" bears spiritual fruit and enables those who follow us to thrive. As you read the following verses that explore ways to cultivate the spiritual "soil" of your life, consider how you are (or are not) "cultivating" and adding "nutrients" in order to create the best "soil" possible. Write down the daily practices and attitudes that are vital to maintaining your spiritual health and a vibrant relationship with God.

Text	Ways You Can Enrich Your Soil	Ways Your Faith Community Can Work Together to Enrich the Soil of Your Community
1 Chron. 16:11; John 16:24; 1 Thess. 5:17	Pray:	
Eph. 1:7; 1 John 1:9	Confess your sin:	
Deut. 8:3; Ps. 119:10–11, 15; John 17:17; Rom. 15:4	Study God's Word:	
Col. 3:16; Heb. 10:25	Worship:	
1 Thess. 5:11; Heb. 3:13	Provide and seek encouragement:	
Deut. 6:1–3; 10:12–13; Ps. 103:17–18; John 14:15; 1 John 2:1–3	Obey God:	
John 14:26; 16:13; Rom. 8:11; 15:13	Rely on the Holy Spirit:	
John 15:1–4; 1 Cor. 9:24–27; Heb. 12:1–2	Fix your eyes on Jesus:	

Text	Ways You Can Enrich Your Soil	Ways Your Faith Community Can Work Together to Enrich the Soil of Your Community
Matt. 22:37–39; 1 Cor. 13:1–13	Love God and other people:	
Matt. 5:14–16; 28:19–20	Be God's witness:	
Prov. 22:6; Eph. 5:22–28	Be committed to family:	
1 Peter 3:10–12; 1 John 3:7	Turn from evil, do what is right:	

Reflection

It's a challenge for many of us who seek to follow Jesus to look beyond ourselves and our spiritual well-being and put effort into nurturing fertile soil within our larger faith community. As Philippians 2:4 reminds us, "Each of you should look not only to your own interests, but also to the interests of others." The work invested for others will build a heritage of rich, abundant spiritual fruit for generations to come.

Take time to read and prayerfully consider what the Bible says about the importance of each of us recognizing our role in the community — the body of Christ:

Just as each of us has one body with many members, and these members do not all have the same function, so in Christ we who are many form one body, and each member belongs to all the others. We have different gifts, according to the grace given us. If a man's gift is prophesying, let him use it in proportion to his faith. If it is serving, let him serve; if it is teaching, let him teach; if it is encouraging, let him encourage; if it is contributing to the needs of others, let him give generously; if it is leadership, let him govern diligently; if it is showing mercy, let him do it cheerfully.

Romans 12:4 – 8

Thoughtfully review your list of ways to enrich your soil and write down how you, in cooperation with others, can help to enrich the soil of your faith community.

Memorize

So in Christ we who are many form one body, and each member belongs to all the others. We have different gifts, according to the grace given us. If a man's gift is prophesying, let him use it in proportion to his faith. If it is serving, let him serve; if it is teaching, let him teach; if it is encouraging, let him encourage; if it is contributing to the needs of others, let him give generously; if it is leadership, let him govern diligently; if it is showing mercy, let him do it cheerfully.

Romans 12:5 – 8

Day Five | God's Community: Repairers of Broken Walls

The Very Words of God

If you do away with the yoke of oppression, with the pointing finger and malicious talk, and if you spend yourselves in behalf of the hungry and satisfy the needs of the oppressed, then your light will rise in the darkness, and your night will become like the noonday....
Your people will rebuild the ancient ruins and will raise up the age-old foundations; you will be called Repairer of Broken Walls, Restorer of Streets with Dwellings.

Isaiah 58:9 – 10, 12

Bible Discovery

Repairing the Broken Walls

In the *ganim*, each garden's fruitfulness — in fact, its survival — depends on the walls of the gardens above it. If one farmer neglects his wall, a heavy rainfall could wash out his garden (wall, topsoil, and crops) and the gardens below. So the farmers of Israel's terraced hillsides learned to work together as a community and to serve one another. If stones tumbled out of a wall, willing hands replaced them. Even today, farmers care for their hillside terraces as a community. After a heavy rainfall, many of them (who may live a distance away) will go to the *ganim* to inspect the walls and repair any weaknesses — not only in their own gardens but in the gardens of everyone else.

IN A *GAN*, THE MOST VISIBLE WALL IS THAT OF YOUR NEIGHBOR'S *GAN*, NOT YOUR OWN. THIS BEAUTIFUL WALL HAS BEEN CAREFULLY MAINTAINED FOR CENTURIES, PROTECTING THE FRUITFULNESS OF THE GARDENS BELOW IT.

1. Those of us who follow Jesus Christ and desire to live fruitful lives that honor God need to view ourselves as repairers
   of broken walls. We must be alert to the needs of people
   around us and diligently work together to rebuild what is
   broken. What needs did the prophet Isaiah identify that, if
   ignored, would tear down and destroy a community? (See
   Isaiah 58:6 – 12.)

   What specific things does God want his people to do that
   would help to repair the walls and bring *shalom* to a broken community? List them! (See Deuteronomy 15:11; Psalm
   82:3 – 4; Proverbs 31:8 – 9; Isaiah 56:1; Jeremiah 9:23 – 24;
   Hebrews 13:1 – 5; James 1:27.)

   Which attitudes hinder us from seeing people whose walls
   are in disrepair and from being willing to help them to
   repair those walls? (See Luke 12:15; James 2:1 – 8, 14 – 16;
   3:14 – 18; 5:5 – 6.)

2. The Bible provides instruction and examples of ways to bring
   God's *shalom* to a broken world. Complete the following
   chart by (1) reading each passage; (2) writing out the guiding
   principle that applies to "wall repair" efforts; and (3) writing down practical ways you can apply this principle to help
   repair and restore the weakened walls in your community.

Text	Guiding Principle	Ways I Can Help
Deut. 22:1 – 4		

Text	Guiding Principle	Ways I Can Help
1 Cor. 13:1–8		
2 Cor. 9:6–13		
Phil. 2:3–8		
Phil. 4:10–14		

Reflection

God's plan is for those of us who follow Christ to be his partners in restoring *shalom* to our broken world. He intends for us to live such good and righteous lives that other people — family members, friends, neighbors, coworkers, people we encounter in our local communities, even people we may never meet — will come to know him. But we do not do this alone. God is in the process of building us up, like well-watered gardens on a hillside, to be a beautiful, fruitful community of Christ followers.

In order to be the community God desires us to be, however, we must have secure walls and fertile soil — not only for our benefit but for the benefit of our community and the larger world. It is our responsibility to tend the community's walls, care for our soil, and partner with God to produce an abundant harvest. If we do not rise up to help heal the wounds in our faith communities, bring peace into our families and communities, love those who are unwanted, and care for those who are in need, then our gardens will quickly become the home of briars and thorns — just like those on many Judean hillsides today. Even a few stones removed from a wall can threaten not only our garden but the entire hillside.

What we think, do, and say affects not only our garden, but the gardens of the community of God's people today and in the future. Every decision we make, every tradition we keep or break in our families, and every minute we spend or do not spend with our spouses and children and friends impacts the soil in the vineyard of God and its fruitfulness in the world. The question we each must ask is: what kind of garden do I want to leave behind as my spiritual heritage?

   In what ways do our modern lifestyle, values, goals, and even our culture itself contribute to the erosion of community — the tearing down of structures that keep a community healthy and productive — in our families and our communities of faith?

What specific things are you doing or will you commit to do in order to become aware of the risks to your community? Meet the needs of your community? Counteract threats to your community?

Who in your circle of influence is at risk and needs help in repairing a wall, and how much effort will you put into repairing that wall?

To what extent are you concerned about your "garden" but ignoring the walls and soil of other people's "gardens" because that is "their" business — not yours?

What changes do you think God desires you to make in your perception and attitude toward other people in need?

To what extent do people who know you consider you to be a "well-watered" garden, and how important is it to you that you be thought of in this way?

How much effort are you putting into keeping your walls and soil in great shape? Into tending the walls and soil of the larger community?

Which disciplines might you need to start, or increase, so that your spiritual life — and the lives of family and friends — have a fertile place in which to grow and produce a fruitful harvest?

Memorize

The LORD will guide you always; he will satisfy your needs in a sun-scorched land and will strengthen your frame. You will be like a well-watered garden, like a spring whose waters never fail. Your people will rebuild the ancient ruins and will raise up the age-old foundations; you will be called Repairer of Broken Walls, Restorer of Streets with Dwellings.

Isaiah 58:11 – 12

NOTES

Introduction

1. Jesus' death (as the Lamb of God) was apparently on Passover; he was buried as the Unleavened Bread festival began, and was raised at the beginning of First Fruit.

2. Since we hold the Bible to be God's revealed word, we reject the arguments of many scholars who do not believe the exodus occurred or at least did not occur as the Bible describes it.

3. A defense of this position can be found in *The Moody Atlas of Bible Lands* by Barry J. Beitzel (Chicago: Moody Press, 1985).

4. A defense of this position can be found in *Exploring Exodus: The Origins of Biblical Israel* by Nahum M. Sarna (New York: Schocken Books, 1996).

Session Two

1. The exact size of a cubit varied from place to place and changed over time but is thought to be approximately 1.5 feet, give or take a few inches.

Session Four

1. As quoted by Jeremy Benstein in an essay titled "You've Got to Be There" in *The Jerusalem Report* (June 2, 2003).

2. "Water in the Desert," *The Jerusalem Post,* May 19, 2006. Rabbi Shlomo Riskin is the Chief Rabbi of Efrat and Chancellor of Ohr Torah Stone Colleges and widely respected. His publications include an excellent two-volume set: *Torah Lights: Genesis Confronts Life, Love and Family* and *Exodus Defines the Birth of a Nation* (Jerusalem: Urim Publications, 2005).

3. I am indebted to the work of Lois Tverberg, author of *Listening to the Language of the Bible: Hearing It Through Jesus' Ears* and cofounder of the En-Gedi Resource Center, for these thoughts. Used by permission.

4. See En-Gedi Resource Center at *www.egrc.net*: "Director's Article," June 2003, and "Biblical Dress: Tassels." See also Jacob Milgrom's

"Excursus 38 on Tassels (Tsitsit)," *JPS Torah Commentary: Numbers* (New York: Jewish Publication Society, 1990).

5. James Kugel, *The Bible as It Was* (Cambridge, Mass.: Belnap Press of Harvard University Press, 1997). Kugel's fascinating book traces many interpretive traditions from their origin in the Hebrew text. On occasion an ancient interpretation or tradition not mentioned in the text of the Hebrew Bible appears in the Christian Testament affirming that the tradition was in fact correct.

Session Five

1. Ron Zvi, "Agricultural Terraces in the Judean Mountains," *Israel Exploration Journal* 16 (1966).

2. I am indebted to Carey Ellen Walsh for many of the insights related to the vineyard as presented in her outstanding article, "God's Vineyard: Isaiah's Prophecy as Vintner's Textbook," in *Bible Review* (August 1998).

Session Six

1. Ron Zvi identified 101 springs in the Jerusalem corridor of the Judean Mountains and 88 more in the Bethlehem and Hebron Mountains. According to his research, more than 85 percent of these were used to irrigate terrace farms, "Agricultural Terraces in the Judean Mountains," *Israel Exploration Journal* 16 (1966): 33 – 49.

2. Bruce Wilkinson, *Secrets of the Vine* (Colorado Springs: Multnomah, 2001). The author provides a helpful discussion of the concept presented here as well as helpful application of Jesus' entire vine teaching.

3. Josephus, *Antiquities* 20.9.2.

4. Nigel Hepper, *Baker Encyclopedia of Bible Plants* (Grand Rapids: Baker, 1992).

5. Leviticus 25:13 – 17. In the Torah God commanded his people to celebrate every fiftieth year as a year of Jubilee. All land which God had given them was to be returned to the family that originally owned it. So if it had been "sold," the sale was not permanent but lasted only until the next Jubilee. Jewish thought saw this as God's way of giving responsibility for a small part of his creation to each family among his people and making them permanently responsible for it. To give it away was to refuse to be responsible for the part of his creation God had given them. To take the field or garden of someone else was to steal from them their opportunity to care for a part of God's world.

ACKNOWLEDGMENTS

The people of God set out on a journey, a journey from bondage to freedom, a journey to the Promised Land, a place flowing with milk and honey. A simple journey, really: leave Egypt and walk to the Promised Land. All they had to do was cross the Sinai Desert and they were there. It would not take long; it was only two hundred miles. But God had another route planned. During the forty years that journey took, the Hebrews, concerned about themselves as we all are, became a community — a people who would put the Creator of the universe on display for a broken world.

The production of this study series is also the work of a community of people. Many contributed of their time and their talent to make it possible. Recognizing the work of that unseen community is to me an important confirmation that we have learned the lessons God has been teaching his people for three thousand and more years. It takes a community. These are the people God has used to make this entire series possible.

The Prince Foundation:

The vision of Elsa and Ed Prince — that this project that began in 1993 would enable untold thousands of people around the world to walk in the footsteps of the people of God — has never waned. God continues to use Elsa's commitment to share God's story with our broken world.

Focus on the Family:

Clark Miller — senior vice president, family ministries
Robert Dubberley — vice president, content development
Paul Murphy — manager, video post production
Cami Heaps — associate product marketing manager
Anita Fuglaar — director, global licensing

Carol Eidson — assistant to business services director

Brandy Bruce — editor

That the World May Know:

Alison Elders, Lisa Fredricks — administrative assistants

Chris Hayden — research assistant. This series would not have been completed nor would it have the excellence of content it has without his outstanding research effort.

The Image Group and Grooters Productions:

Mark Tanis — executive producer

John Grooters — producer/director

Amanda Cooper — producer

Eric Schrotenboer — composer/associate producer

Mark Chamberblin, Adam Vardy, Jason Longo — cinematography

Dave Lassanke, Trevor Lee — motion graphics

Drew Johnson, Rob Perry — illustrators

Sarah Hogan, Judy Grooters — project coordinators

Ken Esmeir — on-line editor and colorist

Kevin Vanderhorst, Stephen Tanner, Vincent Boileau — post-production technical support

Mark Miller, Joel Newport — music mixers

Keith Hogan, Collin Patrick McMillan — camera assistants

Andrea Beckman, Rich Evenhouse, Scott Tanis, Kristen Mitchell — grips

Shawn Kamerman — production assistant

Marc Wellington — engineer

Juan Rodriguez, Paul Wesselink — production sound

Ed Van Poolen — art direction

Zondervan:

John Raymond — vice president and publisher, church engagement

Robin Phillips — project manager, church engagement

Mike Cook — marketing director, church engagement

T. J. Rathbun — director, audio/visual production
Tammy Johnson — art director
Ben Fetterley — book interior designer
Greg Clouse — developmental editor
Stephen and Amanda Sorenson — writers

BIBLIOGRAPHY

To learn more about the cultural and geographical background of the Bible, please consult the following resources.

Anderson, Richard. "Luke and the Wicked Tenants." *Journal of Biblical Studies* 1.1.

Basser, Herbert W. "The Jewish Roots of the Transfiguration." *Bible Review* (June 1998): 30.

Beale, G. K. "An Exegetical and Theological Consideration of the Hardening of Pharaoh's Heart in Exodus 4 – 14 and Romans 9." *Trinity Journal* 5 NS (1984): 129 – 154.

Beitzel, Barry J. *The Moody Atlas of Bible Lands*. Chicago: Moody Press, 1985.

Berlin, Adele, and Marc Zvi Brettler. *Jewish Study Bible*. Philadelphia: Jewish Publication Society and New York: Oxford University Press, 2004.

Bivin, David. *New Light on the Difficult Words of Jesus: Insights from His Jewish Context*. Holland, Mich.: EnGedi Resource Center, 2005. (*www.egrc.net*).

Borowski, Oded. *Daily Life in Biblical Times*. Atlanta: Society of Biblical Literature, 2003. *www.amazon.com*. (Accessed 30 September 2009.)

Bottero, Jean, Elana Cassin, and Jean Vercoutter, eds. *The Near East: The Early Civilizations*. New York: Delacorte Press, 1967.

Clements, Ronald. *The World of Ancient Israel: Sociological, Anthropological, and Political Perspectives*. Cambridge: Cambridge University Press, 1991. *www. amazon.com*. (Accessed 30 September 2009.)

Davis, John J. *Moses and the Gods of Egypt: Studies in Exodus*. Grand Rapids: Baker, 1971.

deGeus, C. H. J. "The Importance of Agricultural Terraces." *Palestine Exploration Quarterly* 107 (1975): 65 – 74. *www.google.com*. (Accessed 30 September 2009.)

_____. "The Importance of Archaeological Research in the Palestinian Agricultural Terraces with an Excursus on the Hebrew Word *gbi*." *Palestinian Exploration Quarterly* (PEQ) 107 (1975).

Dickson, Athol. *The Gospel According to Moses*. Grand Rapids: Brazos Press, 2003.

Edelstein, Gershon and Shimon Gibson. "Ancient Jerusalem's Rural Food Basket." *Biblical Archaeologist* 44 (1981).

Edersheim, Alfred. *The Temple: Its Ministry and Services as They Were at the Time of Jesus Christ*. London: James Clarke & Co., 1959.

_____. *The Life and Times of Jesus the Messiah*. Peabody, Mass.: Hendrickson, 1993.

Elbaum, Leiah. *Plants of the Bible*. Leiah Elbaum, ed. N.p., 2003. *www.geocities.com/jelbaum/plants2002.html*. (Accessed 28 September 2009.)

Feiler, Bruce. *Walking the Bible: A Journey by Land through the Five Books of Moses*. New York: HarperCollins, 2002.

Fleming, James. *The Explorations in Antiquity Center*. La Grange, Georgia: Biblical Resources, 2007.

Fretheim, Terrence E. *Exodus: Interpretation, A Bible Commentary for Teaching and Preaching*. Louisville: John Knox Press, 1991.

Friedman, Richard Elliot. *Commentary on the Torah*. San Francisco: Harper, 2001.

Ginzberg, Louis. *An Unknown Jewish Sect*. New York: Jewish Theological Seminary of America, 1976.

Hareuveni, Nogah. *Nature in Our Biblical Heritage*. Kiryat Ono, Israel: Neot Kedumim, 1980.

_____. *Tree and Shrub in Our Biblical Heritage*. Kiryat Ono, Israel: Neot Kedumim, 1980.

Hepper, Nigel F. *Encyclopedia of Bible Plants*. Grand Rapids: Baker, 1992.

Hillers, Delbert R. *Covenant: The History of a Biblical Idea*. Baltimore: Johns Hopkins Press, 1969.

Hoffmeier, James K. *Ancient Israel in Sinai*. Oxford: Oxford University Press, 2005.

_____. *Israel in Egypt*. Oxford: Oxford University Press, 1996.

Homan, Michael M. "The Divine Warrior in His Tent." *Bible Review* (December 2000).

Jordan, Jennifer "The Wine of Israel and Wine in Biblical Times." Posted 27 October 2006. *EzineArticles.com*. *www.ezinearticles.com/?The-Wine-of-Israel-and-Wine-in-Biblical-Times&id=340401*. (Accessed 28 September 2009.)

Kenneth A. Kitchen. "Tabernacle: Pure Fiction or Plausible Account?" *Bible Review* (December 2000).

Kline, Meredith G. *Treaty of the Great King*. Grand Rapids: Eerdmans, 1962.

Lesko, Barbara and Leonard. "Pharaoh's Workers." *Biblical Archaeology Review* (January/February 1999).

Lesko, Leonard H., ed. *Pharaoh's Workers*. Ithaca, N.Y.: Cornell University Press, 1994.

Levenson, Jon D. *Creation and the Persistence of Evil*. Princeton, N.J.: Princeton University Press, 1988.

_____. *Sinai and Zion: An Entry into the Jewish Bible*. San Francisco: Harper, 1985.

Levine, Baruch A. *The JPS Torah Commentary: Leviticus*. Philadelphia: Jewish Publication Society, 1991.

Milgrom, Jacob. *The JPS Torah Commentary: Numbers*. Philadelphia: Jewish Publication Society, 1991.

Peterson, Eugene. *Eat This Book*. Grand Rapids: Eerdmans, 2006.

Pryor, Dwight. *Unveiling the Kingdom of Heaven*. Dayton, Ohio: Center for Judaic Christian Studies, 2008.

Rainey, Anson F., and R. Steven Notley. *The Sacred Bridge: Carta's Atlas of the Biblical World*. Jerusalem: Carta, 2006.

Riskin, Shlomo. *Torah Lights: Genesis Confronts Life, Love and Family*. Jerusalem: Urim Publications, 2005.

_____. *Torah Lights: Exodus Defines the Birth of a Nation*. Jerusalem: Urim Publications, 2005.

Sarna, Nahum. *The JPS Torah Commentary: Exodus*. Philadelphia: Jewish Publication Society, 1991.

_____. *The JPS Torah Commentary: Genesis*. Philadelphia: Jewish Publication Society, 1991.

_____. *Exploring Exodus: The Origins of Biblical Israel*. New York: Schocken Books, 1996.

Silverman, David P. *Ancient Egypt*. Oxford: Oxford University Press, 1997.

Spangler, Ann and Lois Tverberg. *Sitting at the Feet of Rabbi Jesus*. Grand Rapids: Zondervan, 2009.

Telushkin, Rabbi Joseph. *The Book of Jewish Values*. New York: Bell Tower, 2000.

Tigay, Jeffrey H. *The JPS Torah Commentary: Deuteronomy*. Philadelphia: Jewish Publication Society, 1991.

Turkowski, L. "Peasant Agriculture in the Judean Hills." *Palestine Exploration Quarterly* 101 (1969): 101 – 12. *www.google.com*. (Accessed 30 September 2009.)

Tverberg, Lois with Bruce Okkema. *Listening to the Language of the Bible*. Holland, Mich.: En Gedi Resource Center, 2004. *www.egrc.net*.

Walsh, Carey Ellen. "God's Vineyard: Isaiah's Prophecy as Vintner's Text-book." *Bible Review* (August 1998).

Watterson, Barbara. *Gods of Ancient Egypt*. London: Sutton Publishing, 1996.

Wilkinson, Bruce. *Secrets of the Vine*. Colorado Springs: Multnomah, 2001.

Wilkinson, Richard H. *The Complete Gods and Goddesses of Ancient Egypt*. Hong Kong: Thames and Hudson, 2003.

_____. *The Complete Temples of Ancient Egypt*. Hong Kong: Thames and Hudson, 2000.

Zevit, Ziony. "Three Ways to Look at the Ten Plagues." *Bible Review* (June 1990).

Zvi, Ron. "Agricultural Terraces in the Judean Mountains." *Israel Exploration Journal* 16 (1966).

More Great Resources
from Focus on the Family®

Volume 1: Promised Land

This volume focuses on the Old Testament—particularly on the nation of ancient Israel, God's purposes for His people, and why He placed them in the Promised Land.

Volume 2: Prophets & Kings of Israel

This volume looks into the life of Israel during Old Testament times to understand how the people struggled with the call of God to be a separate and holy nation.

Volume 3: Life & Ministry of the Messiah

This volume explores the life and teaching ministry of Jesus. Discover new insights about the greatest man who ever lived.

Volume 4: Death & Resurrection of the Messiah

Witness the passion of the Messiah as He resolutely sets His face toward Jerusalem to suffer and die for His bride. Discover the thrill the disciples felt when they learned of His resurrection and were later filled with the Holy Spirit.

Volume 5: Early Church

Capture the fire of the early church with the faith lessons in Vol. 5. See how the first Christians lived out their faith with a passion that literally changed the world.

Volume 6: In the Dust of the Rabbi

"Follow a rabbi, drink in his words and be covered with the dust of his feet," says the ancient Jewish proverb. Come discover how to follow Jesus as you walk with teacher and historian Ray Vander Laan through the breathtaking terrain of Israel and Turkey and explore what it really means to be a disciple.

FOR MORE INFORMATION

 Online:
Go to FocusOnTheFamily.com
In Canada, go to FocusOnTheFamily.ca

 Phone:
Call toll-free: 800-A-FAMILY
In Canada, call toll-free: 800-661-9800

BD10XTTWMK

More Great Resources
from Focus on the Family®

Volume 7: Walk as Jesus Walked

Journey to Israel where 12 disciples walked the walk their rabbi Jesus taught them. Examining the culture and the politics of the first century, Vander Laan opens up the Gospels as never before.

Volume 8: God Heard Their Cry

Just when it seemed that Pharaoh could not be defeated, God provided for His people in ways they never could have imagined. Join Ray in ancient Egypt for his latest study of God's faithfulness to the Israelites—and a promise that remains true today.

Volume 9: Fire on the Mountain

When the Israelites left Egypt, they were finally free. Free from persecution, free from oppression, and free to worship their own God. But with that freedom comes a new challenge—learning how to live together the way God intends. In this ninth set of Faith Lessons, discover how God teaches the Israelites what it means to be part of a community that loves Him, and the lessons we can begin to live out in our lives today.

Volume 10: With All Your Heart

Do you remember where your blessings come from? In Exodus, God warned Israel to remember Him when they left the dry desert and reached the fertile fields of the promised land. But in this tenth volume of Faith Lessons, discover how quickly the Israelites forgot God and began to rely on themselves.

FOR MORE INFORMATION

Online:
Go to FocusOnTheFamily.com
In Canada, go to FocusOnTheFamily.ca

Phone:
Call toll-free: 800-A-FAMILY
In Canada, call toll-free: 800-661-9800

BD10XTTWMK

Share Your Thoughts

With the Author: Your comments will be forwarded to the author when you send them to *zauthor@zondervan.com*.

With Zondervan: Submit your review of this book by writing to *zreview@zondervan.com*.

Free Online Resources at
www.zondervan.com

Zondervan AuthorTracker: Be notified whenever your favorite authors publish new books, go on tour, or post an update about what's happening in their lives at www.zondervan.com/authortracker.

Daily Bible Verses and Devotions: Enrich your life with daily Bible verses or devotions that help you start every morning focused on God. Visit www.zondervan.com/newsletters.

Free Email Publications: Sign up for newsletters on Christian living, academic resources, church ministry, fiction, children's resources, and more. Visit www.zondervan.com/newsletters.

Zondervan Bible Search: Find and compare Bible passages in a variety of translations at www.zondervanbiblesearch.com.

Other Benefits: Register yourself to receive online benefits like coupons and special offers, or to participate in research.

ZONDERVAN®

ZONDERVAN.com/
AUTHORTRACKER
follow your favorite authors